THE HAUNTING OF HOLLY HOUSE

A GHOST STORY

CHARLOTTE WEBB

NENE PUBLISHING

For my dear friend, without whom, life would be far less fun and far more difficult.

CHAPTER 1
PRESENT DAY

"Did you think you'd get away with it?" the voice cut between the two girls and they both jumped; their heads whipped around to see where the voice had come from. They both breathed out sighs of relief to see their House Mistress leaning over them with a mischievous grin on her face.

"Mrs Stevens, you made us jump!' Lizzy laughed, holding her hand to her mouth.

Mrs Stevens frowned and stretched her arm out to confiscate the iPad that rested on Lizzy's lap between the two girls.

"Oh," Mrs Stevens commented, perplexed, "I had thought you were watching YouTube or something..."

Lizzy and Emma exchanged a look of raised eyebrows and squished-up noses, which their House Mistress caught.

"...Or whatever it is you girls are into nowadays. But this is – this is a *periodic table?*"

Mrs Stevens looked at them, confused but partially impressed, with one eyebrow raised, seeking an explanation.

"Yes," shrugged Lizzy "I was just showing Emma something interesting I learnt the other day and explaining it to her."

Mrs Stevens and Emma regarded each other momentarily and Emma rolled her eyes in good humour at her friend's academic eagerness.

"Well, this is commendable, girls – it really is. And normally I absolutely wouldn't interrupt an extra-curricular science lesson. But this is not iPad time, as you well know. You're supposed to be devising your plays for the end of term," she switched the tablet off and held it against her chest with her arms folded over it. "I am hoping that Holly House will win the best house competition this year girls!"

"But we can't really, Miss," Emma justified, "Rosie and Dawn are doing that charity event today over in the quad and we can't really start writing the play without their input."

Lizzy nodded in agreement, as Mariah Carey's 'All I want for Christmas' suddenly kicked in on the stereo system, followed by whoops of approval from the other girls dotted around the recreation hall in clustered teams. They were briefly distracted by a girl on the other side of the room who suddenly draped herself in red tinsel and started strutting about miming the words, much to the delight of her raucous friends. Mrs Stevens turned back to Lizzy and Emma, clicking her tongue.

"Well, I'm sure you can make a start. You know the tradition – select any item from the props room under the stage and use this to inspire your story," Mrs Stevens recounted.

"It doesn't seem fair to do it without the others..." Lizzy explained.

"And Hermione will be super-upset if we start doing *anything* drama-related without her," Emma chipped in.

"Hermione?" Mrs Stevens questioned.

"Oh," Emma instantly blushed, "Oh Hermione is our nick name for Rosie...because – well, you know Rosie."

Mrs Stevens brought to mind the studious, conscientious young Rosie who always put her hand up first and was consistently willing to help those who needed extra tuition, then she nodded and smiled. Very like Hermione Granger, she thought as she stifled a laugh.

"Yes. I know Rosie."

Lizzy and Emma shared a conspiratorial smile.

"Well, if you think going ahead with the plot and scripting without them would upset Rosie, then perhaps just select your prop today and do a little brainstorming on ideas," Mrs Stevens gestured towards the looming wooden stage, "the props room will be locked again after this session."

The girls followed her gaze to the low-rise door beneath the stage – usually hidden by wood panelling. When their house matron, Vickie Winter, had opened it half-an-hour ago, she had made silly, spooky ghost sounds to make the girls laugh and roll their eyes at her, as they tended to fondly do with Vickie on a regular basis. There was lots of ghost stories that were told to the first years when they arrived at the boarding house for Meadowbank School for Girls. It was a kind of tradition that proved quite useful at preventing the new girls exploring under the stage without a member of staff. Vickie had to separate a few streams of cobwebs from the passage, luckily enough she wasn't afraid of spiders. She inserted her hand to the inside wall to find the light-switch, which had illuminated the space under the stage, shelves full of colourful paraphernalia, stacked tables and chairs. Clothes rails with costumes hanging, and hats on a hat stand. It hadn't been opened since their summer production in June and different items were extracted then – June was a time for parasols, buckets and spades and fake wooden ice-creams. So far this morning, Lizzy had clocked her peers coming out with props such as a holly wreath, a red Santa hat and a box of artificial snow.

Lizzy shrugged and asked Emma, "shall we?"

Emma nodded half-heartedly and adjusted her socks before coming to stand. Mrs Stevens noticed, not for the first time, how Emma's socks seemed to slightly cut into her rather fleshy ankles – she made a mental note to email her mother requesting she send new socks in the next size up. The poor girl must be uncomfortable – but she wouldn't mention it to Emma; it might give her a complex. Millions of minutiae reminders like these were the fabric that furnished Laura Steven's mind throughout the school term – she looked forward to the festive break in just three and a half weeks' time, when she could concentrate solely on her own life and family for a few weeks, rather than on the sixty daughters of St Ellen's boarding house, none of whom belonged to her. She smiled with satisfaction as she watched the girls approach the props room.

Lizzy picked up an old China doll and blew the dust off it, then rubbed frantically at her nose to stifle a sneeze.

"Urgh. Not that disgusting thing," Emma scrunched up her face, "it's creepy as hell."

Lizzy repositioned it on the shelf where she had found it. "It reminds me of one my grandmother used to have in her spare bedroom."

Emma stopped, whilst reaching for a typewriter. "Isn't that the room I stayed in when I came to visit you at your Grandma Mary's in the summer?"

"Yes," Lizzy affirmed, distracted by her browsing, "but I think the China doll left when she heard you were coming…"

They both turned to face each other and guffawed with laughter.

"What about this?" Emma held up a fire helmet.

"Hmm. It doesn't scream '*Christmas*,'" Lizzy scrunched up her nose.

"Uh, excuse me," Emma sassed, with one hand on her hip, "you know Hermione would be saying *'You need to let the prop guide the direction of the script and not arrive with preconceived ideas...'*"

Both girls laughed as they could hear their friend's voice clearly in their heads.

Lizzy felt drawn away from the shelves to a folded pile of costumes in a wooden chest. As she lifted a red, velvet robe from the top of the pile, a flurry of moths suddenly flew up into her face and she screeched.

"No fooling around with the props girls," bellowed the voice of Mrs Stevens from the cavernous hall. They felt sequestered away and offered no response, as if the outside world had no bearing on decisions made in here, in their own little temporary microcosm.

The moths hadn't deterred Lizzy from the mound of clothes – she lifted them out, depositing them on the dusty wooden floor beside her, muttering about "something underneath."

Emma turned to look when Lizzy inhaled a quick intake of breath and Emma slowly walked towards the item that Lizzy had uncovered.

"Oh wow...." Emma whispered as she came towards it. Lizzy involuntarily took a step back. They both stared at the black and gold writing on the old wooden box for a moment and then their eyes met.

"It's a Ouija Board!" Emma whisper-squealed in excitement and went to reach for it.

Lizzy stopped her hand mid-reach. "No way, Emma. Forget it."

"Oh, come on!" Emma enthused, "it would be the most fun prop EVER. We could make our play a Christmas ghost story! It's *inspired*!"

Lizzy removed her hand from Emma's arm and helplessly watched as her friend lifted the board delicately up and shifted it about in her hands, examining the intricate engravings.

"I don't know...." Lizzy started, but there was more intrigue in it than uncertainty.

Emma turned the board over in her hands and pointed at a gold inscription on the back. They both leaned in, squinting in the half-light.

Emma read aloud: "*Resist the temptation to play with the dark arts. Do not release the spirits of the underworld that lie within.* Oh my God, Lizzy...."

"I know," Lizzy's voice quaked slightly.

"This is PERFECT!" Emma shrieked.

"What? No..." Lizzy was confused by her friend's reaction.

"Everybody loves a ghost story!" Emma

asserted, "quick – let's take it back to our dorm before any of the other girls can take it!"

Lizzy didn't move. "Rosie won't like it," she stood shaking her head.

Emma folded her lips together in a moment of consideration, and then her eyes twinkled deviously as she grinned. "But Dawn will!"

Lizzy bit her lip and reluctantly followed Emma to go, but just before they left Lizzy shouted "wait" and ran back to get the red cloak, "wrap it in this so no one sees it." "Good thinking," said Emma and wrapped it around the board as she ducked at the low door on her way out. They started a half-run which was not quite the pace that would warrant a *'No running inside!'* yell from Mrs Stevens, but which expediated their exit. Lizzy followed behind, keeping pace, and they both skidded down the polished wooden floors of the corridor that led to the grand stairwell. They scuttered up the stairs in hushed giggles – though they learnt long ago that these stairs were impossible to be quiet on. Each one had its own depth of hollow reverberance or thump or creak; they made their passage fast so that any attention attracted would mean they were long gone by the time a Matron had come to check who was running in the halls.

Once upstairs, they ran along the balcony, trying not to knock the holly, ivy and golden bell decorations from the ornate bannisters as they went. As they reached the wing of their dormitory corridor, they allowed their laughter to ring out loud, echoing down the halls along with their thunderous footsteps – they were breathless and joyful.

Lizzy pushed the heavy wooden door to their dorm so that Emma didn't drop the board and when they flung themselves inside, they came to a sudden still, leaning against the door, triumphant that they had made it upstairs without interrogation. They stood side-by-side, catching their breath, their mouths wide open and eyes sparkling with mischief.

When they had regained their breath, Emma uncovered the board, dropping the red cloak on her bed and held the board out in front of her. Wiping some remnants of dust off its surface with her fingers, she said "so what now?"

"Now we have to convince the others," Lizzy grinned through gritted teeth.

CHAPTER 2

PRESENT DAY

"Well, that was dull," Dawn announced as she threw herself face-down on her bed.

"It's good you did it, though", encouraged Lizzy.

"What was it for again?" Emma asked, feigning interest when all she really wanted to do was reveal the thing causing the excitement in her chest.

"Oh, my Mum and Dad," Rosie began, "it's a doctors' thing – a medical research project. They're keen to get Meadowbank School involved in the fundraising." She sighed demonstrably and didn't say anymore.

Dawn pulled her face from the duvet and shook

her head to clear her hair from her eyes – it fell into a perfect, blonde, shiny parting. It always did. Lizzy watched her, thinking about how long she had to spend in the bathroom mirror to get her own parting straight when she created her favourite current hairstyle of two French plaits either side of her head. Yet Dawn's just fell like that naturally. Lizzy would probably feel jealous if she had that in her, but Lizzy's envy never translated in a malicious way; she felt happy for her beautiful friend.

"So, what did you losers get up to while we were away then?" Dawn asked.

Emma stole a glance at Lizzy, eager to share the secret with their friends.

"Oh, not much," Lizzy jumped in "we had to start devising the play…"

"Oh no!" Rosie sounded physically pained, "you didn't start without us?"

"Mrs Stevens said we at least had to choose the prop," Lizzy continued "so we just did that – we didn't start the script or anything."

"Okay," Rosie accepted, sulkily, sitting on the end of her bed.

"I wouldn't be surprised if your Mum and Dad conspired with Mrs Stevens, Hermione," Dawn laughed, "get the drama stuff done whilst she's stuck in our charity bash!"

"Are they still pushing for you to become a doctor?" Lizzy empathised.

Rosie nodded miserably, "that's why we've *got* to make this play amazing so that when they come to see it, I can prove to them that the stage is where I'm really supposed to be, not some GP surgery."

"Sounds ambitious," Dawn countered "I'm not sure they'll be that easily won."

"So, what did you get?" Rosie eagerly turned the topic around.

"Sorry?" Emma stuttered nervously, caught a little off-guard, though she *did* understand the question – it was the one she'd been hoping they would ask from the moment they'd walked through the door.

"The prop," Rosie explained, "it's crucial you got a good prop, as our whole play depends on it for inspiration."

Lizzy could feel the anticipation of the moment coming off Emma in waves. She was practically rubbing her hands together "oh, we got a good one alright!" Emma teased.

Rosie's interest was piqued "oh really? What is it?"

"Yeah, let's see it then!" prompted Dawn.

Lizzy exhaled slowly, resigned to the situation.

Emma excitedly crossed the room to the little cupboard that stood between her and Lizzy's beds; she opened it cautiously and then, with both hands, carefully removed the prop and held it out for Rosie and Dawn to see.

Rosie's expression dropped as soon as she saw it, but Dawn's reaction was the opposite.

"A Ouija Board!? Awesome! Wow – Matron just let you take it?"

Lizzy shot Emma a look.

"Not exactly. We didn't really *ask* her..." Emma cringed "but it was in the props room, we were told to take something, so we took this!"

Dawn laughed triumphantly, "there you go then, Hermione – the BEST prop for your important play!"

Emma grinned at the rapturous reception.

"No, no, no..." Rosie was shaking her head "we can't use that!"

"We won't actually play it, Rosie – it's okay. It will literally just be a prop," Lizzy tried to console her, but Rosie was shaking her head, cowering.

"What do you mean *we won't be using it*?" Dawn bowled in, disappointed.

Emma rolled her eyes in response and Lizzy crossed to Rosie, to rub her arm "it'll be a Christmas ghost story. It will be amazing. And you'll have the main part!"

"Not with that thing, I can't! It gives me the creeps..." Rosie looked up at Lizzy, appealing to her.

"You should have seen the China doll..." Emma muttered under her breath.

"Haven't you guys watched *any* horror movies?" Rosie implored "whenever any character uses a Ouija board, something terrible always happens."

"That's why it'll make for such a good plotline," cajoled Emma.

Dawn stood from the bed and crossed over to where Emma was still holding the board out. She took it delicately from her, inspecting the inscriptions.

"Oh wow," Dawn burst excitedly, reading "*Resist the temptation to play with the dark arts. Do not release the spirits of the underworld that lie within.*"

"I know...!" Emma squealed, thrilled that she wasn't alone in her excitement.

"Oh nooo..." Dawn groaned, simultaneously.

Lizzy sat down on Rosie's bed next to her and comfortably put her arm around her.

"I wasn't the biggest fan of the idea either, to

begin with..." Lizzy empathised "but the props room will be closed now, so we really have to stick with it..."

Lizzy looked towards the window, where it had already begun to get dark. Light from the lamp outside in the garden square glinted on the gold edging of the Ouija board and all their eyes were momentarily drawn to it.

Rosie shuddered "maybe I should move to another group where their play has a different prop..."

The reaction was a unanimous "No".

"We need you, Rosie" Lizzy exclaimed.

"Rosie, you're the only one who can write and act and direct – we'll be a mess without you on board!" Dawn added. Rosie appreciated Dawn using her proper name – she was *Hermione* most of the time now from Dawn, so she knew the compliment was genuine.

"Don't leave us, Rosie – you are gold-dust," Emma chipped in.

They all stood around her, breath suspended, awaiting her response. She looked each one of them in the eye.

"I want as little to do with that board as possible," Rosie asserted, laying down her conditions. They all nodded.

"We *won't*" Rosie fixed Dawn with a stare "be using it ourselves – only in the play."

Dawn rose her eyes to the ceiling and dropped her shoulders in mock-impatience, then closed her eyes and gave a slow reluctant nod as the others looked on.

"And" Rosie continued, "I don't want it staying in our dorm."

The other three all looked troubled by this.

"But there's nowhere else ..." Emma defended.

"If any of the staff find it, they might not let us keep it..." Lizzy offered.

"And that would destroy our production" Dawn dropped the clanger – she knew Rosie's weak-spot.

Rosie side-eyed the Ouija board for a moment.

"Well, if it *has* to stay in here," she acquiesced "it has to be *nearly* out the door – so as close to the exit as possible."

They all looked over at Lizzy's bed that stood next to the main entrance to the dorm corridor.

"Under your bed then, Lizzy," Dawn determined matter-of-factly.

"Oh, you're kidding me..." Lizzy began to protest.

"Or no Ouija board play," Rosie stated categorically, "sorry, Lizzy."

Lizzy huffed and stood to take the board from Dawn, then crossed the room, grabbed the cloak and wrapped it around the board. "Just in case" she said before she bent down by her bed and slid the board covertly underneath. She stood with her hands on her hips.

"Done," she confirmed to them all. "Satisfied?"

"Very!" giggled Emma, rubbing her hands together in glee.

"It's time to go down for dinner – I'm starving," Dawn stated.

"We can find out what props all the other groups have got – I bet we got the best one!" Emma gabbled.

"We must tell them all that ours is a secret though," Lizzy advised "just in case it causes trouble." Rosie fixed her with a worried look. "With the staff I mean, silly…" Lizzy laughed, consoling Rosie, who instantly perked up. "Or we just tell them it's a red cloak" Emma said.

"I do actually have quite a good idea for a plot," Rosie confided. "it's all starting to come together in snapshots in my mind – some of my best stories come to me that way…"

The girls all smiled and exchanged fond glances behind Rosie's back; they were used to her creativity carrying her away and were relieved it was to be no different after the whole 'Ouija board' debacle.

"I want to be the character who gets possessed by an evil spirit…" Dawn joked and made goofy freak faces, with her tongue hanging out at Emma, who giggled.

They all made their way out of the dorm, the festive excitement reignited as the warming scent of mince pies the cook was baking downstairs wafted up to them.

"I'll tell you all about the story and our characters over dinner." Rosie called back to them all as she led the way.

Their high-spirited voices echoed out down the hallway as they switched off the light and left the dorm in darkness.

The girls had been allowed half-an-hour of screen time after dinner and whilst Emma and Dawn had opted to watch 'Survivor' on the lounge screen with most of the boarding girls, Lizzy had watched a BBC programme about Vets on one of the shared iPads and Rosie had decided to use the time on her phone, scrolling for stories about Ouija boards. By bedtime, she wished she hadn't.

"You're really quiet, Rosie?" Lizzy prompted over the top of the most recent publication of her 'New Scientist' magazine.

"Hmm," responded Rosie, "could have something to do with that monstrosity under your bed."

"Don't worry," Lizzy assured her, "we haven't even *opened* the board yet. It's been lying dormant under the stage for years, probably decades, without us even knowing it's there. It's not going to be problematic just because we relocated it. And anyway, remember, we promised – we're not actually going to *use* it."

Rosie was consulting her fingernails, so didn't see the look that was exchanged between Emma and Dawn and the way that Emma winked conspiratorially. Rosie also hadn't heard the whispers passed between them during the screen session earlier in the evening.

"That whole thing about not actually using the Ouija board..." Emma had prompted.

"What do you think?" Dawn had side-eyed her.

"It would be a missed opportunity, wouldn't it?" Emma taunted.

"Hermione doesn't need to be involved if she doesn't want to..." Dawn justified.

"But she can't stop us doing if we do want to..." Emma agreed.

They had shared a mischievous giggle and then gone back to watching the episode.

Rosie sat up in her bed now, having decided to share.

"I don't think you all have a full understanding of how dangerous that thing is."

They listened.

"I heard this story – a woman was grieving after her husband died. They were both young – maybe in their early thirties but he'd been in a car accident and gone through the windscreen. His cause of death was a slit throat from a particularly large slice of dislodged glass. She was desperate to contact him because she just couldn't get past this thought that he had died in terrible pain. So, she and her friend did a Ouija board to contact him, and they asked '*how did you feel when you died? Were you in pain?*' When suddenly, the patio door window blasted inwards at them and a particularly large slice of door glass slashed the woman's throat and she died instantly."

They were all silent.

"At least she got an answer, then" Emma joked to break the tension.

Lizzy picked up her pillow and threw it at Emma playfully. They all laughed – except Rosie.

"See? I knew you weren't taking it seriously," she pouted "anyway I hadn't finished. Her friend then becomes possessed by a spirit – I'm not sure if it was the husband, but something else comes through and she ends up taking some of the broken glass and slashing her own throat with it too. She was brutally injured, but she actually survived it and that's how she's been able to tell what happened."

"Where did you hear this story, Rosie?" asked Lizzy.

"On google…" Rosie responded sheepishly, and they all groaned.

"Your parents are doctors, Hermione! Didn't they ever tell you never to google something you're worried about?" Dawn laughed.

"I'm not doing the play," Rosie huffed and shuffled lower into her duvet, signalling the end of the conversation.

The others looked around at each other in concern.

"Unless I can come up with such a brilliant

storyline that it makes the fear worthwhile," she continued, "and with less blood."

The girls smiled at each other in relief. They all bid one another goodnight and turned off the lights. Then all laid there wishing the light was still on and trying not to think about the thing under Lizzy's bed...

CHAPTER 3
PRESENT DAY

The dorm room was a sudden excitable flurry of energy as Emma and Dawn burst in giggling, slamming the door behind them and throwing themselves on to their respective beds.

"Do you think they'll suspect anything?" Dawn questioned as she tried to catch her breath.

"No," Emma assured her friend "Rosie is too carried away writing the script and Lizzy was going to some science experiment thing in the lab. They won't miss us."

Dawn gritted her teeth through a grin, "shall we get on with it then?" Her eyes zipped over to Lizzy's bed.

Emma stood purposefully, marched over to

Lizzy's bed and dropped to her knees to retrieve the Ouija board from under the bed. She held it aloft, looking about the room.

"We need a flat surface to place it on…"

Dawn grabbed the small desk that sat in the far corner of the room and dragged over two small stools that accompanied it, then placed them in the centre of the room. The desk and stools got used for hair-combing and make-up application activities much more often than they did for homework. There was a mirror on the wall above where the desk usually stood and so it lent itself more to the purpose of a vanity area. Besides, with laptops that could perch comfortably on knees in bed, they had little reason to sit at a formal desk. Lizzy even had a little lap-table she would construct across her legs in bed. Her Grandma Eliza had made it for her; she was a resourceful lady who loved a bit of up-cycling and had always been very handy with woodwork. The girls in the dorm had admired it when Lizzy first used it for her homework and now Grandma Eliza had commissions for three more. But the Ouija board called for a much more stable base and the two girls sat on the stools, facing one another, as Emma set the board down between them. They both sighed, just staring at it.

"Don't we need glasses?" asked Dawn suddenly.

"Oh yes!" Emma jumped up and retrieved two small water glasses from her and Dawn's bedside tables; she emptied any dregs of water into the tiny sink in the other corner of the dorm and brought them over to the table, wiping the interiors of the vessels on her big cardigan so that they wouldn't make the board wet when they flipped them upside down. She passed a glass to Dawn and they both turned them upside down on the tabletop.

"Do you think it needs to be dark?" asked Dawn, once Emma had settled.

"Oh – probably yes..." Emma jumped up again and made in the direction of the window to draw the curtains.

"No! I mean-" Dawn's call stopped Emma in her tracks "Do you think we *need* to? I mean, I'd probably rather *not* have it dark..."

Emma's eyes twinkled mischievously, "Are you scared?"

Dawn shrugged, "A bit. Aren't you?"

Emma tipped her head onto one side, considering the question, "But it's only a bit of silliness, isn't it? It's only a toy."

Dawn's eyes dipped to the board – somehow it seemed dangerous to disrespect it in that way.

"Still," Dawn continued "if we can keep the curtains open...it's nearly three o'clock and the winter nights are drawing in so quickly now, so it'll be dark soon anyway. I don't think we need to make it any darker."

Emma smiled and nodded her understanding. "Okay. Agreed. We'll leave the curtains open. But I'll switch off the light, okay?" She headed over to the light switch mounted near to the door on the wall.

"Did we even turn that on?" frowned Dawn.

Emma looked at her finger on the switch – she couldn't recall switching it on as they arrived at the room.

"I don't know," Emma shrugged, "but either way it's off now." She switched the light demonstrably as she said the word 'off' and it made Dawn shudder a little.

Emma took her seat opposite Dawn once again and they stared at each other, then at the board.

"So, are we ready?" Emma prompted.

"I guess..." Dawn shrugged, and Emma unfolded the Ouija board and positioned it out in front of them. It was a beautiful dark mahogany wood and marked in gold stencil were the numbers one to nine and zero, all the letters of the alphabet, a large 'Goodbye' and then in each corner one of the following: Yes, No, Maybe, Unknown. They both took a few moments assessing the board and then caught each other's eye – Emma with a grin and Dawn with a look of trepidation. Emma picked up her glass, indicating Dawn to do the same, but as she did, Emma started laughing raucously, breaking the tense silence.

"Ha ha! What are we doing? We only need one!" She took Dawn's glass from her hand and placed it on the floor between them.

"Do we?" asked Dawn nervously.

"We're such amateurs!" Emma laughed fondly. Then she tipped the glass upside down on the board and placed the tips of her fingers on top of it, and with her eyes indicated that Dawn should put her fingers on too. Dawn did so and let out a shaky breath.

Emma smiled at her with reassurance but also excitement and closed her eyes, which made Dawn feel instantly alone. If anything happened, she didn't want to be the only one to see it, but she also *really* didn't want to close her eyes – it made her feel too vulnerable. So, she stared instead at Emma's face and tried to mirror her breathing pattern – Emma seemed calm, but Dawn certainly didn't feel it.

It must have been a full minute, when Emma's eyes startled open with such suddenness that Dawn saw her dilated pupils retract.

"Nothing's happening," Emma whispered. Dawn was about to suggest they pack it away, but then Emma suggested, "I think we're supposed to talk, right?"

She didn't wait for Dawn's response, but closed her eyes and dived right in.

"Hello? If there are any spirits here who want to speak with us, we are open and listening...."

Dawn dare not close her eyes and wondered if Emma could feel her fingers shaking.

"We are friendly, and we hope you are too..." Emma added, with a little giggle.

"You can move the glass to point to letters to spell out your message to us...if you'd like..." Emma continued, "or not..."

Something caught Dawn's attention behind Emma – it was as if a cloud crossed the already-weak winter light that was permitted through the window. A shadow cast momentarily across the room, but it was a sudden movement and Dawn felt it must have been her imagination. Emma still had her eyes closed, so she wouldn't be able to corroborate when they discussed it later on and this troubled Dawn for a moment, but then Emma was talking again – for talking's sake it seemed to Dawn.

"So, we got this Ouija board for a play, we're going to devise a story to use it as a prop – maybe you could give us some inspiration, if you can hear us...?"

Nothing.

Emma opened her eyes and looked at Dawn with disappointment.

"Shall we just leave it then? It's getting darker now – we won't even be able to see the letters soon..." Dawn implored.

"One more try," Emma smiled and closed her eyes again.

"Are you there? Won't you talk to us? We're nice young girls, I promise... We're devising this play with our friends, Rosie and Li..."

The glass moved! It *shoved* itself very decisively and Emma's eyes flew open in shock.

"Was that you!!?" But she could tell by the fact that Dawn had grabbed her hand away and how very suddenly pale she had turned, that it was not her that had moved the glass. Emma looked down to see where the glass had been relocated to – it was the letter 'B'.

Emma looked at Dawn in desperation, "Please

put your hand back on, Dawn! We have to see if it moves again!"

Dawn felt very suddenly as though she wanted to cry, but simultaneously that she couldn't step away now things had started to happen – rather like the scenario of a car accident where she was desperate to see if there were casualties involved but also felt sick at the prospect of actually seeing people covered in blood. She tentatively placed her hand back on Emma's.

The glass moved instantly to 'E'.

Dawn's hand flew off again, instinctively.

"Please, Dawn..." Emma pleaded.

Dawn put her hand back on and steeled herself.

The glass whipped over to the letter T, then moved away and went back to T again.

"Wait!" Emma retorted "B-E-T-T...what's it spelling?"

The glass then moved to 'Y'.

"Betty!" Emma yelled in triumph and Dawn removed her hand, needing a break.

"Are you pushing this thing, Emma?" Dawn accused.

"No!" Emma was affronted "I absolutely swear that I'm not!"

Dawn replaced her hand, looking up at Emma through her eyelashes.

The message came in quick succession now and Emma violently yelled out the letters as they came, trying to keep track and follow what they spelt.

"T.E.L.L.H.E.R.I.A.M.W.A.I.T.I.N.G.F.O.R.H.E.R."

They both removed their hands from the glass. Emma seemed suddenly exhausted, and Dawn was just overwhelmed. There was a pause while they figured it out.

"Betty. Tell her I am waiting for her." Emma surmised, then looked Dawn dead in the eye in the half-light.

"Who's Betty?"

"I don't know and seriously, Emma – this 'toy' just got very real. Can we stop now please?"

"But what if Betty is an old lady who lives in Meadowbank village, and we can pass on a message from her deceased husband? It could be the true love of her life trying to contact her!" Emma convinced Dawn, as she placed her fingers back on the glass.

Dawn frowned sadly and replaced her hand on top of Emma's in resignation.

The movement started up again almost instantly and Emma verbalised the spelling as before.

"C.L.A.R.A.K.I.L.L.E.D.R.O.S.E.M.A.R.Y."

Their hands both instantaneously jumped off the glass and Dawn buried her hand in her lap.

"Did it just say Clara killed Rosemary?" Emma frowned.

Dawn shook her head "If there's any kind of killing involved, I'm out of here..."

Emma appealed to her friend "Please – we could be about to solve a murder!"

"How?" Dawn squealed, "we don't know a Clara and we don't know a Rosemary!"

"Just once more, Dawn – then I promise we'll put it away!"

"Only if I can put my hands on the bottom and yours on the top..." Dawn asserted. Emma didn't know if it was because Dawn didn't trust that she wasn't faking it or because she was spooked by the idea of a spirit laying their hands on top of hers to move it, but either way, if they could get more information, she didn't really care.

"Sure," she said and once Dawn had placed her fingers on the glass, Emma joined her for the ride. As soon as the glass started moving, Dawn looked up at Emma in shock as the realisation hit that this glass was absolutely being swept along by something or someone else and that it really wasn't Emma driving it at all. Again, Emma read out the letters:

"C.L.A.R.A.K.I.L.L.E.D.M.E."

The two girl's eyes met over the board as the movement stilled.

"*Clara killed me,*" Dawn whispered, hardly believing what was happening.

The glass began to move again, and Emma sounded out the letters as they came:

"F.I.N.D.B.E.T.T.Y.S.H.E.I.S.M.I.N.E."

The glass stilled and Emma whispered in summary, "Find Betty. She is mine."

They waited and then let their hands fall away as it seemed nothing else was coming.

Suddenly the door burst open, and the two girls jumped in alarm, with Dawn releasing a shrill scream, then covering her mouth with her hand as she registered Lizzy and Rosie standing in the doorway, staring at the set-up in front of them; the desk, the stools, the glass, the Ouija board, the realisation...

"But you *promised!?* You *promised* you wouldn't use it!!" Rosie shrieked into the hush of the silenced room.

"We're so sorry, Rosie..." Dawn began to stand to console her friend, but she lacked the energy and slumped back down into her stool.

"Guys," Lizzy began, taking in the scene, "this is *not cool*."

It was the first time Emma seemed to regret what they had done. She looked up at Lizzy with doe-eyes.

"I'm sorry, Lizzy, sorry Rosie. It was me – it was my fault, my idea. Dawn didn't really want to do it. I led her astray." Emma admitted.

Lizzy could believe it – Dawn was easily influenced, and Emma just didn't engage her brain sometimes. Lizzy reached out to Rosie, to comfort her as she looked entirely betrayed. But where Lizzy had expected Rosie to cry or flounce off down the corridor, she didn't – she placed her hands firmly on her hips and lifted her chin high.

"Well, you'd better have had an incredible experience that I can write about!"

Emma and Dawn shared a moment, appraising each other's faces, before Emma swallowed hard and said "sorry to disappoint, but there's not much to tell. You'll have to use that brilliant imagination of yours, Rosie..."

Dawn's mouth dropped open at Emma's lie and watched as Emma busied herself, folding the board back into place, handing it to Lizzy to replace it under her bed, putting the water glass up by the sink, moving the desk and stool back into place. Then Dawn realised that she would need to also move in order to convince the others that it really had been a non-event. She stood abruptly from her stool, and as it shuffled backwards it knocked over the glass noisily that was behind her stool. The others all jumped at the crash and Dawn stared at the glass in horror. The spare glass that they didn't use. The one that they had placed on the floor *between them* – it was now *behind her*. As she stood wide-mouthed gaping at it, Lizzy mistook her shock.

"It's okay – it didn't break. Look, 'Lizzy picked up the glass, "no harm done."

Dawn closed her mouth and attempted a smile, nodding to demonstrate this satisfied her worries.

By this point, Rosie was settling on her bed, opening her notepad to continue writing the script, still pouting a little at the idea her friends had gone behind her back.

"Look, we really are sorry Rosie..." Emma started, "but I can see you need some space without us two around, so come on Dawn – let's go for a wander..."

Emma grabbed Dawn by the hand before she could protest and the two of them exited the dorm.

"Why did you tell them nothing happened?" Dawn whispered urgently.

"Can you imagine how much Rosie would have freaked out if we'd told her?"

Dawn recognised this as a rhetorical question.

"So the messages we got," Emma summarised, "Betty. Tell her I am waiting for her. Clara killed Rosemary. Clara killed me. Find Betty she is mine."

Dawn stopped walking and leaned against the solid wood panel that lined the corridor. Emma stopped in response and retreated her steps back to Dawn.

"What?" Emma whispered.

"The glass moved," Dawn confided in Emma.

Emma laughed in response, "of course it did! You don't still think it was me!?"

"No.... not *that* glass. The one we didn't use! The one we left on the floor between us. When I knocked it over, it was no longer between us – it was behind me."

Emma's eyes flitted to the side and narrowed, as she tried to remember and visualise the positioning, "oh shit – you're right."

The girls stood in silence for a moment, each of them processing the insanity of what had just happened. Then Emma lurched for Dawn's hand again and pulled her along down the corridor.

"Where are we going?" Dawn asked.

"The library," Emma explained, "there's a whole archive on Meadowbank School for Girls throughout the ages - we're going to look up the history of the school."

As Emma and Dawn sat with large heavy books laid out in front of them and old newspapers which had been filed in plastic to protect them from the damage of ageing, Emma couldn't quite believe what she was reading aloud.

"The staff listing from the year 1875, shows that the Headmistress was Mrs Alice Brown; she employed her sister-in-law, Clara Brown, as House Mistress of St Ellen's Boarding House on the Meadowbank School grounds. Clara Brown was supported by House Matron Rosemary Faulkner who had worked at the Boarding House since its opening in 1863."

Both girls re-read the text silently, before Dawn pulled away with a deep intake of breath, then released it with a shudder. Emma looked at Dawn –

it seemed for once Emma had no comment to contribute.

"There's a Clara. And there's a Rosemary. Just like in the messages we got," Dawn blinked in consternation.

Emma could only nod.

"We have to tell the others..." Dawn demanded of Emma.

"Rosie will freak out!" Emma protested.

"Grab some paper from the printer and a pen from the library desk," Dawn instructed, "we'll write it all out. If Rosie can see a story and we can frame it as an opportunity, she might not be as volatile when we tell her."

Emma shot her a look that said she didn't believe that approach was going to work, but she stood to grab some sheets of A4 from the printer tray and swiped a blue biro from the desk, then settled back in her seat to start writing it all down.

Dawn watched her write and then asked the question that had been niggling at her since the library book had confirmed the names:

"So if Rosemary was killed and Clara was the killer, who else did Clara kill? Who were we talking to?"

Emma paused and looked up at her. "I think there's only one way we can find out..."

"No!" Dawn insisted. "I'm not doing that again!"

"Not tonight," Emma agreed, "but with the others, once they know, there's safety in numbers."

"You seemed so relaxed though, Emma – do you think we're not safe?" Dawn rubbed at her upper arms, feeling suddenly cold.

Emma shrugged, "I always thought I knew what to believe, but I have no idea anymore."

Dawn looked upwards at the tall wooden ornate ceilings and shelves of books piled high enough that the library even had a ladder on a rail so that the upper levels of volumes could be reached. Their whispers echoed here and outside the window; Dawn could see that the day had turned to evening as they had looked through the books. The sky was a sinister purplish-grey and a lone branch scraped against the windowpane each time the breeze buffeted it about. It was early December and freezing outside, but the library was heated, so why were both girls feeling a drop in temperature? Dawn shivered, "My god it's getting really cold in here, Emma can you feel it? It's like a window is open."

"Yes, but they're closed," said Emma, looking

worriedly at Dawn. Both girls felt ice cold and goose bumps began to raise on their arms. "I feel a bit sick and I've got a pain in my chest Emma, can we please go? I'm getting the creeps sitting here..."

"Sure," Emma replied, as she had just finished copying from the book, "let's get back to our haunted dorm room – then we'll feel a lot better." She smiled ironically at Dawn, who tried for a half-smile that didn't reach her eyes. They walked swiftly up the corridor, but Emma suddenly stopped, "oh no, I left the book out, let me run back."

"Ok I will stay here, I'm just warming up, I still feel...." But Emma was gone, running down the corridor. Dawn felt breathless and her heart was pounding. She looked up and down the long corridor; it was warm and well-lit, so why did she feel so scared? In that moment, she heard a blood curdling scream coming from the library- it was Emma. The door to the library banged shut and Emma was running towards her. She was ghostly pale, and terror flashed in her eyes. She was shouting at Dawn, begging her to run.

Both girls arrived in the school entrance lobby too breathless to speak. Just at that moment Vickie came out of the office.

"Are you ok girls?" she said, "have you been running?"

"Yes," said Emma, "there is a man in the library, he wasn't there, and then suddenly he was!"

"What?" said Vickie, "What man, and what were you doing in the library? Its nearly dinner time". Very slowly and very seriously, and in a low voice Emma said, "We were in the library studying, there was no one in there but us, we left, and I had forgotten something and when I went back in, I walked over to the desk where I had left the book, and it was gone. When I looked up there was a man stood right in front of me. Please go and see for yourself, he's in there." Dawn was horrified, and she turned to Emma and looked at her as if she had gone mad. "There was no man in the library Emma, and I know he didn't come in after you as I was stood in the corridor."

"For Goodness' sake, can't you hear what I am saying? There is a strange man in the library!" Emma was shouting now, and Mrs Stevens came out of the office to see what was going on. Before she got a chance to speak Vickie told her that there was a strange man in the library, and both ladies took off down the long corridor.

The dinner bell was ringing, and old wooden stairs started to creak as a stream of girls descended and flowed into the dining hall. Emma and Dawn were leaning against the wall by the office when Lizzy and Rosie come down the stairs. They rushed over to them and asked where they had been. At that point Mrs Stevens and Vickie burst through the door from the library corridor, and Mrs Stevens looked furious. "What the hell were you two playing at in there? Get in my office now! Lizzy, Rosie, you can go for your dinner, now."

EMMA AND DAWN sat with tears flowing down their cheeks, begging Mrs Stevens to believe them. She had found books in multiples of ten stacked in piles on the floor and on desks all over the library.

She was giving them detention tomorrow, which entailed them spending their free afternoon with Rachael the librarian, tidying the mess they had made. They were sent into dinner and then they were to go straight to their dorm without down time that evening. Both girls were pleading but the conversation was over, they were dismissed.

They ate separately as they had gotten to the

dining room late, and there were only a few spaces left on different tables. After dinner they didn't see Rosie and Lizzy, and they both went up to the dorm and sat looking at each other. "What the hell happened?" Dawn asked Emma. Emma reiterated the same story as she had told the matron.

"He was stood there, right in front of me Dawn, he was a huge man, and he smelled of alcohol," Emma went on, "he scared the hell out of me, he reached out to touch me and I turned and ran as fast as I could. There were no books piled on the floor or desks; I just don't understand. How could that of happened in just a few minutes. From us leaving the library to them going back must have been five, maybe ten minutes."

"I was terrified in the library Emma, I think I was having a panic attack, my heart was racing, and I felt sick, there was something in there, something evil." Dawn was trembling, Emma could see it.

"Oh, Dawn I am so sorry, I know you said you didn't feel well but I thought you were, well exaggerating."

"Do you think it's the Ouija board?" Dawn asked hoping the answer would be no.

"We need to tell the others; they need to know." Emma was suddenly very forceful in her tone. "Ok, but Rosie won't want to do the play and-''. Dawn didn't have time to finish her sentence before the door to the dorm was flung open.

"Do you think we'll have turkey every day in December?" Lizzy rolled her eyes as she made her way through the dormitory door and slumped down on to her bed.

Rosie grasped at her stomach "Urgh. Too much stuffing..."

"Oh hello, are you two ok? Where were you at dinner? What did you get called in to the office for?"

Dawn eyed Emma pointedly.

"Emma has something to tell you..." the seriousness of Dawn's tone alarmed them all and they all turned to look at her. Dawn raised one eyebrow suggestively at Emma, causing Lizzy and Rosie to turn to Emma, whose face was ashen. Emma nodded, "Well we have something to tell you."

"Okay, yeah. Listen, guys – sit down..." Emma gestured to them all to perch on the ends of their beds, which bought them all together into a cosy square – it was their default 'sit and chat' positioning, but the girls could tell that what Emma had to say carried more weight than her usual banter.

"Urgh…" Emma looked at Dawn for help.

"We weren't exactly truthful earlier, when we said that nothing had happened when we tried the Ouija board…" Dawn explained.

Rosie visibly stiffened, "What happened?"

"It was really funny…" Emma attempted, jostling them along, but the attitude wasn't contagious.

"It was weird," Dawn began, "really weird."

"I've written it all down…" Emma pulled a piece of folded white paper from her pocket and carefully straightened it out, "this is going to be amazing content for the play, Rosie…"

Rosie looked thoroughly unconvinced.

"We received four messages -" Emma began to tell.

"What?" Lizzy looked excited. In honesty, she really hadn't imagined anything would be picked up. She stole a look over at Rosie, who she felt protective of, but also couldn't quell her intrigue.

"So the name that came up was 'Betty,'" Emma continued.

Lizzy took a sharp intake of breath, and the other three girls looked at her expectantly.

There was a beat of silence, then Lizzy laughed, "A name! I mean – that's cool it gave you a name straight off, right?"

The others blinked at her and returned to the piece of paper.

"It spelled out these messages: *Tell her I am waiting for her. Clara killed Rosemary. Clara killed me. Find Betty she is mine.*" Emma finished and looked up into the eyes of her friends. Dawn looked quite relieved to have shared, Rosie looked awestruck, and Lizzy seemed agitated.

"But it makes no sense!" Rosie assessed, "we don't know any Betty, Clara or Rosemary – do we?"

"Well," Emma shot Dawn a knowing smile and referred to her paper, "we went to the library to do a little research on the history of the school."

"And in the archives for 1875, it says..." Dawn gestured for Emma to continue reading from the paper.

"That the House Mistress for St Ellen's was called Clara Brown. That one of her Matrons was called Rosemary Faulkner..."

"Bloody hell!" Rosie stood up, surprised and unsure what to do with herself.

Lizzy had gone very still, "And Betty? Is there a Betty...?"

"None that we could find," Emma confirmed.

"Were there any murders documented?" Lizzy interrogated.

"We didn't look much longer after we found the names – something really weird happened." Emma and Dawn explained everything that happened. Emma described the man in such detail, "He was a very tall man, with sharp facial features, dark eyes that pierced into me." It was hard for any of them to disbelieve her. "He was there, he must have been hiding in there all along, that's the worst thing! Maybe he was watching us? He could be some kind of pervert." Emma was getting angry now, in place of the fear she had felt at first.

"Then the weirdest thing of all," Dawn spoke now, "Mrs Stevens and Vickie went to the library to see who was there and they said the books were stacked on the floor and on the desks, but there was no man in there. We didn't stack any books, but we are getting detention and must go and put them all back with Rachael tomorrow." Dawn said sulkily.

"We need to do the board again!" Lizzy announced and the three other girls stared at her aghast.

"What?" Emma frowned, "But you never wanted to do it in the first place!"

"What if there's a warning for this *Betty*? What if there's a murderer and after Clara and Rosemary, Betty is next?" Lizzy gabbled.

Dawn looked between her friends, partially amused, "Lizzy, if somebody murdered those women in 1875, then the murderer is very dead by now – it was nearly one hundred and fifty years ago!"

"Oh, okay, well..." Lizzy looked down into her lap and fiddled with her fingers, "I just feel like there was obviously some message trying to get through and we don't have the full story."

Lizzy appealed to Rosie, "This could really help the plot – if we find out who Betty is and what really happened here..."

Rosie was already shaking her head, "There is no way we're opening that board again, Lizzy. You can forget it."

Lizzy bit at the inside of her mouth and looked down – she could feel that nobody in the room was particularly keen on exercising more spirits tonight.

"And how are we supposed to sleep now, knowing that all of that happened today in this very room?" Rosie asked, pulling her dressing gown on over the top of her clothes.

Dawn smiled deviously "'*Friends.*' One episode of Chandler, Joey, Monica, Phoebe, Rachel and Ross will sort us out.'' Dawn pulled her laptop out of her bedside drawer and pulled up YouTube as the others piled onto her bed to watch.

Somehow, they had all managed to fall asleep. It had probably been the adrenaline rush that had drained them and as the four of them slept soundly in the silent room, a shaft of moonlight fell across Lizzy's bed through the small gap in the curtains in the otherwise dark dormitory. Though she did not move, her bedsheets began to peel away from her as if they were being pulled down. In her sleep, Lizzy moaned and turned onto her side, shivering. The coldness woke Lizzy and audibly shuddered with complaint as she sat up to lean forward and retrieve her bedding from where it had bundled up at her feet. She snuggled down into the duvet, pulling it tight up under her chin, smiling comfortably as she appreciated the warmth, but the smile faded as – despite the warmth of the covers – she felt an icy coldness creep over her. She opened her eyes to check whether the door had been opened or the window. Neither had, but the chill that came over her felt as cold as the December air outside. She blew into the air through pursed lips and saw a cloud form. She wondered in her sleep-fogged brain whether the school's heating system had perhaps broken – but how could this be the case, when she was warm and snuggled just moments before? As she lay there, trying to figure out why the room had gotten cold so suddenly, her duvet began to slip down from where it was tucked under her chin, down to her chest. It was weird, because her duvet wasn't slippery; it was a heavy bulky winter set that usually held firm. She wriggled it back over her, unable to bear the frigid cold. Then it began to move very deliberately away from her – even as she held on to it, there was a force pulling it in the other direction and as she let go in shock, her whole duvet was flung off of her to the end of the bed, exposing her to the cold and to the voyeur; whoever or whatever it was. Even as the phrase entered her head, it sounded alien and absurd, but she *felt* it – she felt vulnerable and violated. As the duvet landed at the foot of her bed, she released a shriek – it wasn't intended nor even a conscious action; Lizzy was most definitely not a screamer. But every atom of her instincts yelled out.

A bedside light was instantly switched on by Rosie and both Dawn and Emma were talking over one another; "what's the matter?" "what's happening?" "Lizzy, are you okay?"

"Check under my bed!" Lizzy demanded; convinced that somebody was in the room, someone who had pulled her duvet from her and was now hiding, "There's somebody under my bed!"

The girls looked at each other in concern.

"We should get Matron!" Rosie stated, but even as she did, Emma marched over to Lizzy's bed, flipped up the fallen duvet and bent down to take a look under the bed.

"There's nothing there," Emma confirmed, "just the Ouija board."

The girls all exchanged nervous glances, then Emma turned to Lizzy, who was pale and shaking, "I think you had a nightmare, Lizzy..."

"No! It was real...it got freezing cold and then something was pulling my bed covers from me, I swear..."

"But it's warm in here," Dawn crossed to the large, wall-mounted cast iron radiator, touching it and whisking her hand quickly away, "the heating is on full blast."

Emma sat next to Lizzy on her bed and placed her palm to her forehead, "You feel cold. Perhaps because your duvet fell off? You got really cold, and it gave you a nightmare...?"

Lizzy shot Emma a warning look. "I know what happened, Emma."

Emma sighed and looked to the others, "Doing the Ouija board was a mistake – I get that now."

"But it's not like a spirit could have *come out* of the board, is it?" Dawn reasoned, "we put it away – it can only talk to you whilst you're playing with the board."

"Dawn's right," Rosie acquiesced, "so long as you've said *'goodbye'* on the board, it essentially closes off any channels that spirits can use as medium."

Emma and Dawn's heads turned quickly to look at one another. Rosie noticed.

"Guys, you *did* say goodbye when you were using the board, didn't you?"

Their panicked expressions told her all she needed to know.

"Oh, my God – that's the golden rule! I can't believe it!!" Rosie's usually calm voice was laced with anger at their stupidity.

"But you and Lizzy came in and interrupted the session – we didn't expect you. We just finished up..." Emma tried to justify.

"Yes – I think if we'd been ending it on our own, we would have thought *'oh, how do we end it?'* and the Goodbye would have been pretty obvious to us..." Dawn added.

"Oh, so it's not your fault for *playing* the bloody Ouija board to begin with, but it's mine and Lizzy's fault for *interrupting* you!?" Rosie snapped.

"I didn't mean that..." Dawn groaned.

Lizzy's voice was quiet when she spoke, but the calmness of it broke through their chaos. "What happens when you don't say Goodbye, Rosie?"

They were all quiet. Rosie looked uncomfortable and cleared her throat.

"It leaves the door open to the spirit world. If you don't say thank you and goodbye, the conversation hasn't been closed – so they're still here..."

The four girls shuddered.

"We have to go back on the Ouija board now then and say goodbye" Lizzy insisted.

"It's too late," Rosie whispered "it must be done at the same time; in that session, otherwise we've basically invited them in. Invited them to stay." She sounded so desperate in that moment, as if something had happened that could never be undone.

"Well, I don't know if I believe all the silly superstitions that comes with it, but the messages earlier *were* super weird, so I don't think I'm going to be sleeping much more tonight..." Emma decided.

"It's five AM anyway," Dawn yawned "we may as well watch some more 'Friends' until it's time to get dressed."

They all moved over to Dawn's bed, the furthest away from Lizzy's and snuggled together, trying to forget the messages, to forget Clara, Rosemary and Betty – and whoever it was that was trying to get their attention.

CHAPTER 4
1875

"There is a large pile of socks to be darned in the utility room," Clara's voice barked from the other side of the pantry. Rosemary and Julie jumped – they hadn't seen Clara enter.

"Of course, Ms Brown – I'll get to it as soon as I've finished re-stocking the shelves with the delivery," Julie called back.

"Hurry up about it. I want them done today, Julie," Clara yelled before departing.

Julie rolled her eyes and Rosemary laughed good-naturedly.

"Honestly, I wish you'd got the post and not her," Julie grumbled, "you're so much nicer and all the girls adore you. They hate her."

"Now come along, Julie," Rosemary encouraged, "hate is a strong word. Clara may not always be the easiest person to get along with, but she's very efficient and if Mrs Brown considered her the best candidate for the job, then I'm in no place to judge that decision."

"Oh, come on, Rosemary – you know as well as I do, she only got the House Mistress job because her sister-in-law is the Head Mistress. There's no way she'd have been employed for the role otherwise. You're obviously the stronger candidate but she got it purely because of her family connection."

"Whatever the reason, Julie, she's our Senior and we must respect her," Rosemary clarified.

"But you've been here twelve years working your fingers to the bone, doing a brilliant job of it and then she swans in like she rules the roost. It gets my goat, it does," Julie grumbled as she reached to slide some tins onto the top shelf on her tiptoes. Rosemary fetched the step-block from the corner of the pantry and passed it to Julie. Julie smiled a *thank you*. "You're just illustrating my point there, Rosemary."

Rosemary smiled and picked up the heavy basket of wet washing she had just retrieved from the laundry room and continued her journey on through the pantry out the back door to the beautiful green lawns. George had done an excellent job on keeping them well this season – the borders were beautifully trimmed with fuchsia and magenta coloured Rhododendrons. Rosemary breathed in the fresh scent of the garden and smiled as she admired the flawless blue sky. She enjoyed spring and hoped it wouldn't be long before the rose garden on the east lawn was in full bloom and that George wouldn't be averse to the idea of her collecting petals to make her signature rose scent perfume. He made her nervous and she wanted to put off asking him until the roses were ready – she somehow felt he'd suggest she owed him something if she secured that favour. Rosemary didn't like being indebted to anybody and not to a man like George, whose eyes roamed freely and without inhibition. She tried not to be around him too often; he set her on edge.

This was her favourite chore, scooping wooden pegs from the fabric bag she had made herself and hanging the clean white sheets out on the line to billow in the sunshine. There was a sudden crash of doors opening and out of the dining room spilled an excitable group of young girls, leaving their lunch for some well-deserved break time in the sunshine. Rosemary paused to watch them, smiling at their energy and vitality. She recognised them as the fourth form group, the vivacious Betty and her best friends Pamela and Eileen. They were such a friendly bunch of girls – happy, eager to learn, obedient, and pretty too. Rosemary felt they would all go far in life with those attributes, but in particular Betty, with her long red hair and piercing blue eyes. As the girls skipped over to the garden area, Rosemary could see George Stone's potting shed in the distance and he was there leaning against the wall, watching the girls as well. But he watched them differently. Rosemary assessed his face, unnoticed by him. He was a very tall man, with sharp features, which were currently set in a smirk, a glint in his dark eyes. Rosemary considered his broad, muscular frame, toned by all the hard garden work he tended to on a daily basis. He had rugged tanned skin from being exposed to the sun every day for the past five years that he had worked as the gardener at Meadowbank School. She supposed he was handsome, but there was something hard and unkind about him. She couldn't question his abilities as a gardener to the school, the grounds always looked stunning, but she did question the attention he paid to the girls. He seemed to align his breaktimes with the time the girls came out for recreation time or would often place himself working on the borders near to the tennis courts when the girls were practicing physical education. Rosemary wondered if she should mention it to Clara, as House Mistress – she would be able to escalate it to the Headmistress should she feel it was appropriate to do so.

Suddenly, George seemed to notice her. He straightened up and Rosemary busied herself with the washing again, trying to look as though she hadn't been looking at him, but as she checked back to make sure he wasn't coming over, he blew her a kiss. It wasn't friendly; it felt lewd. Rosemary was affronted and clicked her tongue to herself. She would definitely need to mention him to Clara.

Rosemary was struggling to sleep. Jessica Boyd had a temperature and had been in and out of her dormitory feeling unwell; it was Rosemary's job to be there if any of the girls felt restless. It made her happy to do so, particularly at the beginning of term where they were generally unsettled at being away from home. It was well known throughout St Ellen's boarding house that Rosemary gave the best hugs and comfort, so it was always her they went to – never to the House Mistress Ms Brown. On top of the disruptive nature of the evening, Rosemary was muddling through how she might approach the very *un*approachable Clara with her concerns about the gardener, George Stone. She decided to warm some milk downstairs in the pantry to help her to get sleepy and settle her anxiety.

Rosemary lit her lamp and trod the stairs slowly and carefully, purposely avoiding the boards she knew were creaky – the result fashioned a sort of dance across the landing and Rosemary silently chuckled to herself when she realised how funny she would look should one of the children look out at her from their dormitory. She made it downstairs onto the solid parquet flooring, which wouldn't betray her footsteps if she travelled on tiptoe. It was unlikely she would wake anybody as she walked down the corridor towards the Kitchen, but the silence didn't promote humming or singing – something she was prone to do as she moved about the school and particularly as she sorted the post; it was a happy activity seeing how the children had received letters from their parents and family members, so she always sang as she distributed the mail into the appropriate alphabetized pigeon holes. But tonight, it was too late for singing and she had to consciously stop herself. She was about to push open the door to the Kitchen when there was a hushed commotion coming from the dining room – hurried footsteps, murmured whispers, a woman's giggle and then the distinctive gruff tones of a man's voice trying to be quiet. But men were not permitted in the girl's boarding house and Rosemary was shocked at the thought that one of the lovely girls she looked after might betray her trust by sneaking in a boy from the village, so she began to march towards the couple, who had now made it to the dining room door, which opened up on to the sweeping gardens and pushed the door noisily open, in amongst further hushed giggles. Rosemary paused at the sight of their two silhouettes as the couple embraced in a parting smooch, because this was no fifth-year student with a clandestine meeting – these were two fully grown adults. The woman was quite voluptuous, and the man was tall and broad. Rosemary watched, unseen, as the man loped across the lawn towards the potting shed and the long-limbed half-run was instantly recognisable to Rosemary as the covert and awkward movements of a certain Mr George Stone. It was only as the woman locked the doors behind him and went to turn that Rosemary realised there was no way she wouldn't be seen and would need to speak now in case she should surprise the woman and risk a scream in the night.

"Clara – Ms Brown -" Rosemary stepped into the room assertively, despite her heart thumping madly; her lamp illuminating her face.

The woman gasped and her hand flung to her chest "Rosemary Faulkner, how dare you sneak up on me like that!"

"I was just fetching some milk from the ..." Rosemary was wrong-footed by Clara's anger.

"I was feeling a little unwell. I needed to get some fresh air," Clara lied, fixing her hair which had fallen messily on one side of her head.

Rosemary took a breath. "I saw George Stone, Ms Brown."

Clara assessed Rosemary for a moment through the darkness.

"Whatever are you talking about?" she snapped, defensively.

"I just saw George leave and go back across the lawn...and unless the rules changed recently, I believe no male company is permitted within St Ellen's." Rosemary allowed the accusation to hang there between them.

"You're quite right, Rosemary – the company of men is strictly forbidden, and I'll thank you not to make aspersions on my character. I am well aware of the rules, and I live by them as if I wrote them myself," Clara declared haughtily, "you were clearly sleepwalking and dreamed the whole thing."

Rosemary remained in silence, weighing up how to advance the situation.

"Besides," Clara continued, identifying a new angle, "you are aware – are you not? That I lost my own dear husband just five years ago. It's insensitive of you to suggest that my heart may have healed enough to allow another man anywhere near me!" As Clara seized upon this narrative, she became increasingly impassioned, "why, I should report you to Mrs Alice Brown for your disrespect and audacity!"

Rosemary cowered at the suggestion, terrified that she would lose her job, which meant all the world to her.

"Please don't do that! I did nothing wrong – I was merely collecting some milk to help me sleep..." Rosemary pleaded.

"And you saw nothing?" Clara dictated.

Rosemary hung her head, angry and shamed, "I saw nothing," she repeated through gritted teeth.

"Very well," Clara hissed, "go to bed, Rosemary. I'll need you up at five o'clock sharp to mop this dining room floor before the children are awake for breakfast."

"But why?" Clara stammered, "it was just washed today..."

As she watched in the moonlight, Clara lifted jug of milk and poured it on the floor, "it's filthy," Clara concluded, "Five AM, Rosemary. Good night."

And with that, Clara marched past Rosemary, close enough to clip her shoulder with her own.

Rosemary stood alone in the darkness for a moment and as she heard Clara's footsteps on the stairs, she let out a wounded bleat of distress. Despondently she returned to her bedroom and sobbed.

The day that followed was not an easy one. On very little sleep, after the stress of the evening's confrontation, Rosemary was up early, cleaning the dining room floor. At breakfast, where the staff would take turns to dine, Clara requested Rosemary make her a fresh pot of tea since hers was tepid. She then provided Rosemary with a handwritten list of items to fetch from the village shop, on top of her daily chores and activities which had already filled her entire schedule. Rosemary tried – as she always did – to put a rosy spin on things when they felt bad. She re-framed the inconvenient trek to the village shop as an opportunity to stretch her legs on a beautiful spring day. She applied a smile to her face, grabbed her wicker basket and left the boarding house, taking the path which snaked past the rose gardens so she could see how soon they might be ripe for her perfume making. As she rounded a curve in the pathway, she heard George's voice, just around the corner, and stopped in her tracks. He was talking in a low voice and instantly, Rosemary cursed herself for stumbling upon yet another of his and Clara's trysts. She made to turn and head in the direction from which she had just come, to avoid another awful situation, but as she did so, she heard another voice – and it wasn't Clara's.

"But I've never had any wine," said the noticeably young, female voice.

"That's why I'm inviting you. It'll be a lovely treat – just for you. You know in France, the children drink red wine from a very young age, with their dinner each evening," Rosemary heard George drawl.

Rosemary stepped out from behind the tall rhododendrons "Madeline Wilson?" Rosemary adopted her best authoritarian voice, addressing the girl and avoiding George Stone's eye.

Madeline Wilson visibly crumpled at the sight of Rosemary, "sorry Miss Faulkner."

Rosemary maintained eye contact with the girl and said kindly, "What are you sorry for?"

"Um..." the girl looked between George, who had straightened up and begun pruning the hedge with some shears that were in his hands, as if he had nothing to do with the situation playing out. "I think I'm supposed to perhaps be in Chemistry..." Madeline blurted out.

"Right then," Rosemary nodded, "hurry along, won't you?"

Madeline stole one more quick glance at George, who ignored her and continued pruning, before she turned and ran off towards the Science department.

Rosemary considered saying something to George, but couldn't imagine it being productive, so continued on her way, when she heard his shears stop cutting and he grumbled, "sticking your nose in where it's not wanted again, are you?"

Rosemary was surprised by his tone and by the comment.

"I beg your pardon. Is there something for me to be sticking my nose into?" Rosemary retraced her steps back towards him. George responded with an amused grunt.

She mentally analysed his comment; *Again*. That suggested that Clara had reported to him that they had been caught out by Rosemary the previous night.

"Madeline Wilson is fifteen years old, George. And she is supposed to be in Chemistry. It is not appropriate for you to be keeping her from class." Rosemary wasn't sure how specific to be, so she opted for the safer reprimand rather than anything more suggestive, which she believed should be directed towards George's seniors in the echelons of the school system.

"Duly noted," George huffed with an infuriating smirk on his face. He didn't look at Rosemary and this disregard prompted in her some sense of bravado; she decided to seize the moment.

"George, I would like to take some rose petals once the rose gardens are in full bloom – would this be acceptable to you?"

Now he looked at her and cocked an eyebrow, "Of course, Miss Rosemary. I'll pick them myself for you and you can come and collect them from me in my potting shed," he leered at her.

Rosemary physically recoiled, "that won't be

necessary, George. I will pick them myself, but I wanted to get your approval before doing so."

"Very well," he returned to the hedges, still with an irritating grin on his lips, as if she amused him.

"Good day," Rosemary nodded curtly and then walked briskly off down the path towards the school gate.

Once she arrived at the little shop, Rosemary pulled Clara's list from the pocket on her apron and began to read the items required:

White shoelaces. Rosemary's shoulders sagged. This wasn't the sort of shop that sold shoelaces, and Clara knew it. They would need to make a trip to the main town of Meadowbank for that and visit the cobbler. She looked for the next item: Tennis Racket. Rosemary rolled her eyes. This was all a trick. Clara knew Rosemary wouldn't be able to buy rackets at the local newsagents. She continued to look at the list of unattainable items: Red Shoe Polish, Length of Rope. Rosemary impatiently replaced the list in her apron pocket and turned to walk back to the school with an empty basket.

Rosemary's day wasn't looking to getting any better. She had retired to the small flat she shared with Julie when they were both on duty, for a little rest before the dinner service. Her head was starting to hurt from all the negativity she was feeling. She sat down at her small desk by the window to write a letter to her grandmother, Hetty. It was times like these that Rosemary wondered what it would have been like if her parents had not both died when she was so young – would she be writing to them instead of Grandma Hetty? She always envisaged that she and her mother would have been particularly close – as Hetty was her maternal grandmother and was practically her best friend, it made sense that it would be this way. But she had no way of knowing. Rosemary had been with her grandmother when the fire had broken out in the barn her mother and father were working in on their small farm in the green undulating fields of Oxfordshire. They had tried to save the livestock and ended up inadvertently sacrificing themselves. It was on low days like these that Rosemary recalled the tragedy – most days she managed to push it all to the back of her mind. Besides, many people had lost their parents, and you didn't see them all moping about the place. She was grateful to have such a loyal and loving guardian in her grandmother, so she dipped her quill into the ink well and set to work writing her feelings down.

Suddenly, there was a commotion on the

landing of the floor below – Rosemary could hear the unmistakable bellowing of Clara and protestations of some of the older students. Rosemary placed her quill back in the well and ran to the landing, looking down over the balcony at the kerfuffle.

"I cannot believe you would break such an important school rule! Your impertinence is astonishing!" Clara was yelling and Rosemary could see that she was holding a girl by her collar. Rosemary quickly took the steps, carrying her long skirts bunched in her hand, so as not to trip. Clara had been known to raise a hand to the girls on extreme occasions and Rosemary hoped to intervene before it escalated. As she reached the landing, she was surprised to see that the girl being reprimanded was Betty Grainger – who was tipped to be Head Girl next year. Betty was certainly spirited, but Rosemary couldn't imagine what she could have done to have attracted this sort of humiliation.

"Ms Brown," Rosemary interrupted, flinging herself in amongst the gaggle of girls, "what is it that Betty is supposed to have done?"

Clara raised her free hand, in which she held a bottle of red wine, "This!!"

Rosemary gasped.

"I just found *this* in Betty's section of the wardrobe," Clara confirmed.

Rosemary looked to Betty in surprise, "Is this really yours, Betty?"

Betty hung her head, staring at her shoes and nodded solemnly.

Rosemary looked to Clara, knowing that her punishment would be firm. She was met by a steely stare and pursed lips.

Rosemary gently laid her hand on Betty's shoulder and dipped her face to meet her eye, "Who gave you the wine, Betty?"

"That's a leading question!" Clara yelled, "the child patently procured it herself."

"How could she have done?" Rosemary appealed, "the village shop wouldn't sell wine to a child of Betty's age, and she can't attend town without supervision."

Clara harrumphed and crossed her arms about her chest, "wicked children find a way."

Betty's bright blue eyes regarded Ms Brown with fear at this remark, "I'm very sorry," Betty whispered, tears pricking her eyes, "I haven't drunk any of it."

"Not yet you haven't!" Clara reprimanded.

"What will her punishment be, Ms Brown?" Rosemary was almost afraid to ask.

Clara seemed to consider this with relish, then a thought visibly occurred to her, and she swallowed hard before replying.

"She will stand in assembly to apologise for letting down her teachers, her peers and the school," Ms Brown prescribed.

Betty's head dropped again, but Rosemary found herself wondering that the punishment did not sound as harsh as she had expected. She looked to Clara in surprise. Clara looked dismissively back at her and then marched off down the hallway. It occurred to Rosemary that Clara may be covering for somebody who might be inclined to introduce alcohol to a child... and that if she didn't want Betty to speak up any more about the matter, it might be to her benefit to treat the child more favourably.

Rosemary looked to Betty, who was now staring at her with wide, wet, frightened eyes. For all her confidence and popularity, it was moments such as these that Rosemary was reminded these were merely children in almost-adult bodies.

"That could have been a lot worse," Rosemary warned and watched as Betty's eyes filled with tears.

"There, there," Rosemary bundled Betty into a hug, cradling her smooth head in the palm of her hand, as a mother would a daughter. These poor girls – so in need of their mothers at such an impressionable age; Rosemary could relate to navigating those sensitive teenage years without parental guidance. It seemed so harsh to expect them to make mature, sensible decisions when they didn't have the people there who were supposed to be setting the boundaries. Rosemary did not judge the parents – they often served in the forces or worked abroad and knew that it was a better option for their child to grow up with a consistent environment and a solid British education. Recently, the usual needlework and cookery classes for girls had been joined by innovative lessons such as maths and science – it was such an exciting time to be a girl and if these young females were not in England, it seemed unlikely they would ever have the opportunity to learn these topics and receive the opportunities afforded to them as a result of this education. So, Rosemary understood, but it still stung when she considered that these girls had to wait for Easter or Christmas for that much-needed hug from their mother.

In Betty's case, Rosemary knew, her mother was a successful stage actress – she'd heard that she had the striking looks of porcelain skin, strawberry hair and piercing eyes that Betty had inherited, along with a charming presence and angelic singing voice. Betty's Father was a businessman who worked in the Iron industry. Even when he was based in their London home, as a man, he would never be expected to care for Betty whilst her mother graced the west end stage; therefore, a boarding school was the perfect option for the family.

Betty was a happy child. She had about her a wild freedom; a curiosity and taste for adventure. Rosemary didn't want the school system - or Clara, specifically, to quash that spirit and dampen her down. Rosemary hugged Betty a little tighter as the gathered group of pupils noted the end of the entertainment and melted away back into their respective dormitories.

Rosemary whispered, "You can tell me who gave you the wine. I won't give any names away to Ms Brown."

Betty pulled back from the hug and looked up into Rosemary's face, "It was just a friend."

Rosemary smiled sadly and nodded once, releasing her embrace.

"Write an apology script for the assembly," Rosemary offered the advice kindly, "it will be easier

– you will be able to look at your notes instead of at the audience and it will satisfy Ms Brown that you have given your indiscretion due thought."

Betty bowed her head, whispered "thank you" to Rosemary and disappeared into her dorm, like a ghost of her former self.

Rosemary watched after her and sighed heavily.

Whilst she hated feeling negatively, she really couldn't wait for the day to be over. She lifted her skirts to trudge back up the flight of stairs to her room, mentally noting that she would no longer have time to write to her grandmother, for her break time was nearly over and she would need to head to the dining room soon to assist with student support during the dinner service.

Finally, it was time for Rosemary to end her shift and allow herself to sleep. Dinnertime had been no better – Stella Jonas had spilled an entire jug of milk onto the floor, so there was not only milk to mop, but shattered glass to sweep and a quarantined section of floor to collect sharp smithereens from and divert pedestrian traffic around. It had been a horrible day and that was a rare thing for a cheerful soul like Rosemary, who always made the best of things, so she felt the disappointments more keenly when they did come along. Rosemary sipped from the glass of water at her bedside and went to check at her window before bed – she had been told rain was forecast by an old man in the village who often predicted how the weather might turn, and she hoped rain *would* fall, to encourage along the roses in the gardens that would be the magical ingredient for the summer scent she was desperate to create to lift her spirits, so she risked a peek outside her curtains to see if the pane was spattered with raindrops. Sadly, it was not, but as she looked, there was a loud grating noise from below and a light spilled out onto the grass. Rosemary's room was directly two floors above the dining room, and she recognised the sound of the doors scraping against the concrete, then watched as a very tall man kissed a familiar voluptuous house mistress before scuttling across the lawn to his potting shed. Rosemary shook her head in disgust at the pair and clicked her tongue as she berated her own timing. Then she swished the curtains back into place before George could turn and see her watching, further weaponizing him for future altercations. It would appear their trysts were a nightly occurrence. If Rosemary hadn't stayed up later writing that letter to her grandmother, if she'd fallen asleep at a more agreeable hour, if she'd not been checking for rain – she might have avoided seeing that unfortunate tete-a-tete. As she laid in her bed, she wished she hadn't seen it – if, as it appeared, this was a regular occurrence, she knew she would eventually be called to report it to the Headmistress. This was something she did not want to do, for many reasons – firstly, because she did not consider herself to be a tattle-tale; secondly because she had felt that appealing to Clara's conscience as she had last night regarding the house rules *might* actually help to change her mind and thirdly, because Mrs Brown was Clara's sister-in-law. They shared the grief of Mr Damien Brown – Clara's late husband and Alice Brown's younger brother and as a result were firm, loyal friends. Not only would this seem like an absurd accusation regarding Mrs Brown's dearest sister-in-law, but it would also be a brutal betrayal to the memory of her darling baby brother and Rosemary really did not want to stir up the ugly feelings this would most certainly arouse. Rosemary audibly groaned at the prospect of reporting Clara's nocturnal visitations to Mrs Brown but knew that it was a necessary evil. Otherwise, she countered, she was enabling a prohibited man to roam St Ellen's boarding house at night. A man who was known to be married to sweet Susannah Stone, a seamstress from the village who was quiet, but well-liked. A man who was father to a young daughter barely breast weaned. A man who looked outside of his marital bed for thrills and extra-curricular excitement. A man who was vulgar in his crude observations regarding the females around him, regardless of their age, it seemed. A man who stationed himself far too close to the tennis courts with opportune timing. A man who encouraged young girls to drink wine. A man who watched the fifteen-year-olds as if they were prospective wives lined up for his selection. A dangerous man.

Rosemary screwed her eyes up tight. It may mean her ultimately having to say goodbye to the job that she loved; that she was born to do - it may mean saying goodbye to the wonderful children within her care – she hated that it may come to this, but she had to make peace with the risks - she knew what she had to do.

THE FOLLOWING day presented no opportunity for Rosemary to speak with Mrs Alice Brown about Clara and her clandestine meetings with George

Stone. The Headmistress had been called to several meetings and – upon requesting her availability from the school secretary – Rosemary learned that it would not be a productive time to have such an important discussion, jammed in between stressful appointments. In truth, she was relieved by the realisation that today would not be the day for the talk. In the stark light of day, Rosemary wondered if she had been over-dramatic in her tired state of last night. Was George *actually* a threat? Could Clara perhaps find happiness with him longer-term and therefore, should Rosemary be interrupting their romance? Another few days to consider her options was very welcome. Clara scheduled Rosemary on her most-hated chore today – the quarterly inventory of medicines and placing orders with the pharmacist for renewed generic painkillers and antiseptic for the boarding house. It was a tedious task with no interaction with the children – Rosemary was a sociable soul, and it stifled her to spend the day shut up in an office going through dusty boxes and thin paper forms. She accepted that it had to be done and was generally happy to pick up the slack on the less appealing chores, but it smarted that she knew she had expressed to Clara, not two weeks since, how she hated the medical inventory.

Clara had put her on the job on purpose and it made Rosemary resent it all the more. But now the sun was setting and after this night shift, tomorrow would be her day off. The girls were now mostly all in bed and Rosemary decided she needed an early night. She was just pulling her covers up to her chin when she heard the familiar screech of the dining room door below her. She froze – should she look? It could cause more trouble. Yet she needed to know – if Clara was risking the safety of the girls in the boarding house on a nightly basis, she would have to sacrifice some of her day off tomorrow to go and speak with the Headmistress about it. Rosemary quickly darted to the window and folded over an edge of the curtain to peer out. She saw, as expected, George Stone – except that he was standing outside his potting shed, raising a glass to somebody across the lawn outside the dining room. Rosemary leaned forward to glimpse – not Clara as she had expected - but a shorter, slimmer person, with a long dark plait over pink pyjamas. It was Theresa Crane – a Fifth-year student. Theresa waved a farewell back in George's direction and then entered the dining room and closed the door awkwardly behind her. Rosemary inhaled in shock – George had been entertaining one of the students in his potting shed, with alcohol at nine-thirty in the evening! As she stared, the shock of the situation made her forget her usual discretion and George spotted her – he brazenly raised his glass to her up in her window, with a leering grin. Had the man no shame? Rosemary would need to speak to somebody about this – but not the Headmistress, she resolved – she should approach Clara herself about it. If Clara was beginning a relationship with this man, she certainly would not be happy to hear that he was involving himself inappropriately with female students and she would likely be on Rosemary's side – in fact the heartbreak may fuel her to report George to the Headmistress herself. Rosemary decided this was most definitely the best course of action and on feeling, for once, certain about what she needed to do, she slept soundly for the first time since the night she found out about Clara and George.

Rosemary woke to the sound of Julie being sick in the bathroom. She noted that it was nearly time to wake for the breakfast service, should it be a working day – as it was her day off, it signalled the end of her shift; she was no longer the matron to call if any students needed her. Julie was. Rosemary made her way to the bathroom and – once she had heard the vomiting dissipate – knocked, asking her friend if she was okay.

"Ough," Julie groaned as she looked through a narrow gap in the door at Rosemary "my nephew Fred had this stomach sickness at the weekend – I'm afraid it looks like I've caught it. Don't come too close..."

Rosemary obediently took a step back, "I'll take your shift today, Julie. Go back to bed."

"Oh no, I can't do that..." Julie was readying her long hair into a hold at her neck, preparing for the next vomiting bout which threatened to arrive at any moment, then she darted across the bathroom.

"You can't work being sick. You'll spread it around the whole boarding house, and nobody will thank you for that..." Rosemary confirmed, "besides, I could do with being around today – there is something I need to sort out..."

Julie managed a 'thank you' in between stomach convulsions and Rosemary went to dress herself quickly, ready for breakfast service and for a probable tricky day ahead.

. . .

During the breakfast shift, Clara seemed agitated; even more so than usual. Rosemary found herself dreading the discussion she needed to have even more than she was initially. Once the girls were in lessons, Rosemary went about her day as usual, feeling a little more tired and very slightly resentful at the fact she should be resting or taking a quiet stroll into Meadowbank, perhaps to take afternoon tea in Milly's Tearoom and to post the letter she had written for her grandmother. She went to check in on Julie to see how she was feeling, only to find their sharer-flat empty and later be told that they had sent her home, concerned that a stomach virus could spread like wildfire amongst the students if she stayed. Clara had remained flustered and unobtainable all day – usually this would suit Rosemary as her interactions with Clara were rarely pleasant, but needing to talk to her today made this an annoyance which punctuated her day each time a potential opportunity was scuppered by a child appearing or an unexpected event stealing Clara away.

Late afternoon, whilst the girls had their free period, Rosemary had delivered the line-dried bedsheets to the linen cupboard, having taken them down from the pegs where they had billowed in the spring garden breeze all day. Then she took on rug-beating duty. This was a worse chore in the winter when the girls would trudge in their muddy boots, but during a dry spring, it was a dusty job and as the heavy rugs had to be slung across the washing lines to be beaten with the broom, this had to be done *after* the washing had been taken in. There was a small window of opportunity before darkness or rain came – whichever appeared first. So, once one of the kitchen maids, Bethany, had helped her to lug the hefty rugs over the washing line which hung between the outer wall and the dining room bracket, Rosemary found herself red-faced and more than a little dusty, thwacking the broom continuously at the large doormat relocated from the entrance hallway and now hanging in the garden, when she heard a little yelp. She paused - happy for the excuse to momentarily stop. There was no more sound, so she continued to beat the rug with the broom, coughing as a cloud of dust enveloped her, when all of a sudden, she saw, across the gardens, the door to George Stone's potting shed fly open and somebody dart out, flinging themselves across the lawn, whimpers of protestation escaping her mouth. Rosemary was shocked to find that she was looking at a red-haired, tall, slim, pale skinned girl.

"Betty!" Rosemary cried out instinctively.

The girl's face sought out the voice and diverted her route from the dining room doors where she was originally headed, to now hurtle towards Rosemary, with a wounded cry.

Rosemary dropped the broom and opened her arms for the girl to run into, as she simultaneously witnessed George appear at his potting shed door, looking for the girl. He visibly startled as he saw Rosemary clock him and then shiftily disappeared back inside his shed.

Betty nearly bowled Rosemary over with the ferocity of her hug. Rosemary embraced her and smoothed her beautiful red hair down over her head, sssh-ing her in a comforting, maternal way.

"He tried...he tried to touch me..." Betty gabbled through tears, sobs and snot.

Rosemary abandoned her post by the rugs, pulling Betty alongside her as she hurried her towards the safety of the house.

"Come inside, child. Let's go somewhere you can calm down and you can tell me all about it..." Rosemary rushed Betty up to the third floor and into the little study area she usually shared with Julie in their compact flat. She sat Betty down in a large, cushioned armchair. She wanted to offer her some hot chocolate to calm her nerves, but this would require her to go back down to the pantry and would allow the child time to devise more structured thoughts – Rosemary needed to know the raw detail of Betty's encounter now, before time and distance from it changed the narrative. So instead, she fetched the girl a glass of water and broke off a row of the Fry's chocolate bar her grandmother had sent her. Betty's eyes lit up as Rosemary handed it to her – chocolate was a rare indulgence and just the presence of it seemed to slow Betty's breathing. Rosemary pulled up a stool opposite the girl and leaned in.

"Now have a drink of water. Take a bit of chocolate and tell me what happened…"

Betty took her time savouring the taste of the chocolate and looked up into Rosemary's eyes with such an expression of sadness and shame, it made Rosemary's heart surge.

"I suppose it was my fault really…" Betty's voice was thick from crying.

"No!" Rosemary reached out to hold Betty's wrist, "I don't know what happened in that shed, but whatever it was, it was certainly not your fault. George Stone is a man nearing forty years old; he's over six foot tall and he has a duty of care towards all the pupils in this school. If he did anything to frighten you, Betty, that is entirely his responsibility, and I won't hear a word to the contrary."

Betty swallowed hard, seeming to accept this as a fact.

"So, tell me..." Rosemary gently encouraged.

"It was Mr Stone who gave me the wine that was hidden in my closet," Betty began and fixed Rosemary with a look, to gauge her reaction.

Rosemary merely nodded, closing her eyes briefly, demonstrating that this had confirmed her suspicions.

"I've been to his potting shed a couple of times... he asked me a few weeks ago if I've ever tried wine – he told me that in France, children drink wine every night with their evening meal and that it's really not the naughty thing everybody makes it out to be – that we should be allowed to enjoy it, just as the adults can..."

Rosemary took a deep breath and exhaled slowly.

"So, I went to his shed last Friday during free period, and he gave me some red wine to drink. I thought he was kind – introducing me to an exciting experience that most grown-ups keep us from."

The way Betty said *grown-up* melted Rosemary's heart, reminding her how young the girl was, despite her mature appearance. It was such a dangerous time in a young girl's life – their blossoming body betraying their tender, adolescent minds.

"The red wine made me feel all warm and fuzzy," Betty continued, "and he was so funny. When I think back to the things he said, I suppose they really weren't that funny – not at all – he seemed a bit stupid really, but the wine made everything seem light and uncomplicated and he felt like my Father the way he was so intent on making me laugh and concentrating on me as if I was the only important thing in the world. And I miss my father, you know…" Betty paused to breathe out with a tremor, manifesting the emotion that threatened to erupt. Rosemary nodded comfortingly and smiled, urging her to go on.

"At dinner that night, it was very hard for me to keep from giggling – every time anybody said anything, it seemed hilarious to me…" Betty shrugged.

"Was that the evening Ms Brown reported you for being disruptive and had you clear the dishes as punishment?" Rosemary offered.

Betty nodded, embarrassed, "Yes. Then I

dropped a dish and made her angrier…That's why. The wine."

Rosemary smiled sadly.

"Then Mr Stone called me over as I was playing tennis, to say if I wanted my own bottle of wine to share with my friends, I should come and collect it on Sunday evening. So, I did. He wanted me to stay and open it with him. He said he didn't drink wine, but that he had some gin he would drink and I could also try - but I had promised Hetty I would help her with her needlework assignment, so I couldn't stay – but I felt terribly guilty about it and he said it was quite rude to accept a present and then not spend time with the person who had gifted it to you."

Rosemary's grip on the girl's arm tightened in empathy.

"He made me feel really bad and then he caught me by the tennis courts this morning saying I owed him some company in exchange for the wine. I apologised to him that the wine had been confiscated because I had been caught with it - and he looked really mad, then said that I definitely owed him in that case. That I should come to his potting shed during free period today…so I did…"

Rosemary rubbed at Betty's arm and Betty released a shuddering exhale.

"He was very happy to see me to begin with, when I arrived – all smiles and making jokes. Although they weren't funny ones. I tried to pretend I was laughing, but I really wanted to leave. It just felt awkward and uncomfortable. He offered me some wine, but I didn't want any wine after the trouble it had already caused me. So, he insisted I tried some gin. He didn't *offer*, he *insisted*."

"How did he *insist*, Betty?" Rosemary prompted.

"I said I didn't want any and he said I should really try. And when I said I *really* didn't want any, he came over to me and..." Betty began to breathe faster, unable to reach the words.

"It's okay..." Rosemary soothed.

"He brought the bottle to my lips and with his other hand, he tilted my head back...I tried to move away, and he grabbed my ponytail, then yanked my head back," Betty sobbed, back in the moment, "it spilt down my chin and onto my frock – look..."

It was only now that Rosemary noticed the white frilled neck of Betty's blouse was wet.

"And then...?" Rosemary nudged Betty slightly with her thumb.

"He stood," Betty continued, "he was angry. And he was too close to me. I felt his belt buckle rub against my upper arm – there was no need for it. The potting shed looks small from the outside, but there is plenty of room inside. There was no need for him to rub against me like that. And then..." Betty started breathing very heavily and increasingly fast. Rosemary worried that she might hyperventilate.

"Chocolate..." Rosemary prompted. She had no idea how or why the stuff calmed people down, but the sweetness always seemed to do the trick. Betty took one bite and then another and her breathing regulated. She nodded at Rosemary, signalling that she was happy to go on...

"Then he pretended to fall..."

"Fall?" Rosemary was confused.

"Yes. He was standing to the side of me and then it was as if he well, pretended he was drunk or something and he fell forward – his hand slid down the inside of my leg and his face fell upon my lap and he sort of – *buried his face down* in my lap, breathing in, then pulled back, apologising. But it wasn't real. The whole thing felt staged. He paused too long there in my lap before recovering with an apology. I was shocked – I couldn't move. And he wasn't drunk – it was more of a *dive* than a fall. It was horrible, he held on to me. I leapt to my feet and told him to get off me. He acted like I was mad, saying '*I fell – I can't help it if I fell.*'"

"That was probably the yelp I heard?" Rosemary queried.

"You heard me?"

"I think so..."

"And then I stood and ran for the door, he grabbed my arm, but I managed to get free and that's when I saw you across the lawn..." Betty met Rosemary's eyes, "I'm so relieved you were there. You were just the person I needed to see. Thank you."

Rosemary took small comfort from the fact that she had been a lighthouse in Betty's moment of need. She couldn't believe how George Stone had violated the girl's private space in that way – how he had acted in a brutal, disgusting way and betrayed the trust of the school. Her spine shivered with the urgency of reporting him. She felt sick with the thought that if she had only done so before now, she could have spared young Betty the trauma of what had just happened to her.

"I'm sorry," Rosemary whispered, "I'm sorry for all of it..."

"Will I have to speak to Mrs Brown the Headmistress?" Betty asked, biting her lower lip.

"Possibly," Rosemary nodded apologetically, "but leave it with me and any reporting you need to do, if you need my support, I will absolutely be there with you, through it all – okay?"

Betty sniffed and nodded.

"I like your home," Betty smiled slightly, looking about herself, "and you're a very kind person."

Rosemary smiled back at her and escorted her back to her dorm room with instructions to forget the needlework and bible-study; only to sleep and come to see her if she was struggling with anything. That if she couldn't sleep, she should come and knock at the door of the third floor flat, and Rosemary would be there for her. Betty thanked Rosemary with a generous hug and then entered her dorm, leaving Rosemary standing in the corridor shaken and worried about what would come next...

Rosemary took a deep breath and then knocked on the wooden rickety door. She had never been to the potting shed before – never had any reason to attend. Betty was right though; standing here it seemed larger already than it looked from way across the lawn, where Rosemary usually saw it. He should be in – he would usually be here having his tea at the time the girls ate dinner. Rosemary had not even excused herself from the beginning of the dinner service; this mission had taken full priority. She knew that Clara would be furious with her, but right now she didn't care. The *only* viable priority right now was to start righting some of these wrongs.

Eventually, after a second firm knock, Rosemary heard a masculine groan and then a wooden creak from within. She pushed back her shoulders and held her head high, angling her face to reach the height at which she knew he'd stand when he opened the door – tall, intimidating. She was determined he would not subdue her. As he peeked around the side of the slowly opening wooden door, he was taller even than she had anticipated, and she adjusted the angle of her head accordingly. His expression shifted from one of frustration at having been disturbed, to distinct distaste at seeing Rosemary standing there.

"Disappointed I'm not Clara, or a young, innocent schoolgirl you can manipulate?" Rosemary shot at him before he could speak. She was surprised at herself – she hadn't planned what to say, but this antagonistic vitriol burst from her instinctively.

His frown burrowed deeper still, and he huffed at her with loathing. His breath was rank smelling;

stale, with a hint of alcohol and Rosemary involuntarily took a step back.

"What do *you* want?" George barked at her, putting a particular emphasis on 'you' as if she were some repulsive insect only fit for squishing.

"Stay away from Betty!" Rosemary felt her foot stamp as she said it.

George feigned confusion, "who's Betty?"

"The girl you plied with alcohol, George. The girl who you insisted spent her precious time with you. The girl you tried to grope and made cry…" Rosemary spat her words out.

George looked over her head, around at the gardens as if she was a mere inconvenience to his evening. Then, once she had finished her rant, he looked down at her with total disregard and said, "you sound like a mad woman. You *look* like a mad woman. Your mind is warped."

"I'll tell Clara!" hearing the desperation in her own voice stung Rosemary – she sounded as though she'd lost control.

George smirked and shrugged, "then she'll agree that you sound like a lunatic."

Rosemary sucked in her cheeks and felt her face burn with fury "you are not safe to be around the children. I will be reporting you to the Headmistress."

George smiled at her, seemingly amused by her outburst, then he shrugged "okay," and went to close the shed door, before pausing and adding, "it would be a shame for you though, to end up in the sanitorium because Clara and her sister-in-law don't believe your insane-sounding stories – or worse, if *I get to you* before the men in white coats do…" he raised one eyebrow at her and then slammed the door in her face.

Rosemary was left standing, shaking with anger and she knew she needed to use this energy and adrenaline to begin the justice that needed to be served. She marched towards the dining room – the doors were open to release the smell of food and because it was a warm spring evening. She walked purposely towards the back of the hall, where the matrons and mistresses surveyed the room and carried out various tasks. She was relieved to see Clara standing with her back to the trays, not engaging in any tasks for once.

"Ms Brown," Rosemary addressed her as she approached, "I must speak with you quite urgently."

Clara looked affronted "well, I can't – it is dinner

time. I need to be here assisting service. As should you be."

"It is regarding the misdemeanours of Mr George Stone," Rosemary added, in the knowledge that Clara would not be able to delay this conversation.

Clara's mouth pursed as if she had tasted something sour. Her eyes narrowed as she looked upon Rosemary, then she spun on her heel in the direction of the corridor.

"My office," Clara instructed tightly.

Once they reached the office, Clara checked nobody was in the corridor on either side and then shut the door firmly. Rosemary noticed how much the office had changed since Clara's predecessor had departed – Miss Lucas used to invite people in warmly, with pink scatter cushions on a corner armchair and a mess of notepads and papers about the place. Now it was regimented with dark volumes of encyclopaedias lined up on the shelves and there was a bench made up with a starched pillow and green scratchy throw – Rosemary frowned at it, realising this is where Clara must accommodate George, as it would be too risky to escort him up several flights of stairs each time, she invited him in. Rosemary closed her eyes momentarily to gather her strength. When she opened them, Clara was standing impatiently before her, with her hands on her hips, a confident stance with her feet wide set.

"What did you want to discuss?" Clara demanded.

"Firstly, let me say that I am aware you have some sort of relationship with George – with Mr Stone - and so it is with regret that I must bring you this news..." Rosemary began, but Clara interrupted, "I assure you I have nothing but a professional relationship with Mr Stone, but do get on with it..."

"Mr Stone has been giving alcohol to some of the girls at the school," Rosemary blurted out and tried to read Clara's facial expression but noted no change.

"Furthermore," Rosemary took a deep breath, "I have just this moment been comforting a young girl who fled from George Stone's potting shed screaming and crying, after he pretended to fall on her and then groped her as he did so."

Clara flushed a little and Rosemary witnessed a weakness in her eyes, but then Clara appeared to compose herself and rolled her eyes to the ceiling, "Oh Rosemary, have you not yet learnt how *dramatic* these girls can be?"

Rosemary shook her head – she would not have

this encounter denied "It was not a drama. I saw the event with my own eyes."

"You saw George *grope* the girl?" Clara raised her eyebrows, with mock bemusement.

"No..." Rosemary clarified, "I saw her run across the lawn, leaving his shed..."

"Being dramatic," Clara confirmed.

"No – he touched her in an inappropriate way, Ms Brown! This must be investigated!" Rosemary wanted to stand so that Clara was no longer looming over her, monopolising the power, but she knew that to stand would be to escalate the confrontation and she really needed Clara on her side for this.

"Rosemary," Clara's voice softened, and she stooped to kneel at her level in a patronising way, "between you and I, it is not news to me that George Stone is a drinker – it could even be said that he is a man who struggles with his levels of alcohol consumption. It is something I have been aware of and have been trying to help him with, as a friend, colleague and confidante. I suspect this is why you have jumped to unfortunate conclusions to suggest that there is some sort of romance between the two of us, but I can assure you that this is not the case and that I have been merely a professional, assisting one of the campus staff through a rough patch." Clara pulled up her mouth at both corners, but it could not constitute a smile. She nodded and then continued, "George *does* fall. When he is inebriated – which I have witnessed on a couple of occasions recently – he does lose his balance a little. It is likely this is what happened when Betty interrupted his private evening time. He would surely have been embarrassed that she intruded on his private space – what was the girl thinking? They do tend to flirt with George, the senior girls, as the only real man on the school grounds. It's hard for him to manage their attentions - he doesn't like to be rude, but then they make up cruel stories such as this and threaten to get him into trouble. It's all just an unfortunate incidence that he happened to fall when Betty came to call on him...the deluded child has jumped to wrong conclusions..."

Rosemary just stared at Clara for a moment, before whispering, "I didn't tell you it was Betty..."

Clara was visibly flustered and came to a sudden stand, before crossing her office to fill a glass with water from a jug sitting on the sideboard.

"I assumed," Clara gabbled, "because Betty doesn't stop talking about him...she's obviously entertaining some flight of fancy with regard to George -"

The other way round, Rosemary realised *George won't stop talking about Betty.*

"And the wine I confiscated from her wardrobe – she stole it from George" Clara ran excitedly along with the story that presented itself in her head, "that is probably why she was visiting again this evening – trying to steal another one from him."

Rosemary took a deep breath and stood up, smoothing down her skirts.

"I have absolutely no doubt," Rosemary spoke calmly, "that if you truly believed Betty Grainger was a thief, you would have reported her to the Headmistress and had her expelled from Meadowbank School with immediate effect."

Clara's mouth fell open, unsure how to respond.

"This only confirms to me," Rosemary continued, "that you know exactly what George Stone is capable of – and indeed, what he is doing. I suggest that you are blinded by his attentions and desperate not to upset him. You are enabling him to seduce the young girls in this school because he appreciates you all the more when you don't question him..."

Rosemary realised too late that she had allowed

her anger and resentful narrative run away with her – and that Clara's face had reddened with fury.

"You should be in dinner service, Rosemary Faulkner. This is the very last I expect to hear of your fanciful stories and vexatious lies. Get out of my office now before I speak to my sister-in-law, to ask her to remove you permanently from Holly House Boarding House."

Rosemary gulped hard, denying the tears that bubbled up in her throat. She had always cried when she felt angry and it had constantly been a frustration to her – she wanted to yell and vent, but instead she would end up blubbering into her handkerchief, looking weak. Perhaps though, she countered, this was a blessing right now -the threat of tears stopped her from shouting at Clara and bringing about certain suspension from the school's staff.

Instead, Rosemary dipped her head and scuttled out of Clara's office, feeling the waves of anger rippling off Clara's body as she passed her at the door. As Rosemary made her way back to the dining room, she already knew that her sunny, enjoyable days at Meadowbank School would soon be coming to an end, because this was a bigger issue than her own feelings and she vowed that she would not let the matter rest.

CHAPTER 5
PRESENT DAY

It was Saturday morning, all the girls had a full day off any duties apart from play rehearsals, apart from Emma and Dawn who had been told to meet Mrs Winter the school librarian in the library to put the books away, that they had been accused of stacking in odd places!

"Emma, Dawn," Lizzy called, seeing her friends coming up the library corridor towards her, "have you finished in the library already? I thought you would be there all day putting the hundreds of books back where they should be?"

"Yes," said Dawn, "we met Mrs Winter at 8.30am but when we got there, Mrs Winter had just opened the door to find all the books were exactly where they should be."

"What!" Exclaimed Lizzy, "who put them back?"

"I think Mrs Stevens and Vickie might have played a joke on us?" Dawn said, "Although not a funny one," Emma chimed, "in I was genuinely scared, I really did see a man in the library. Maybe they thought I was messing around, but I know what I saw."

"Well, you can find out now if you like, we have been asked to go to see Mrs Stevens". "Mrs Stevens wants to see us. *Why* does she want to see us?" Dawn asked.

"Does she know about the Ouija board?"

"I genuinely don't think she does..." Lizzy assured her three friends as they made their way hurriedly down the corridor that led to the Housemistresses' study, "she said she's speaking to all the teams to ask how their production is coming along."

"But we've hardly started!" Rosie cried in dismay.

"So, we tell her so," Dawn shrugged, "honestly, the less information we can give her on our play, the better."

"Let's be vague about the prop -" Emma suggested in a whisper as they arrived at the office door. They all nodded, seeking out each other's eyes for agreement.

Lizzy suddenly turned to look behind her.

"What is it?" Rosie asked – she'd noticed that Lizzy had been jumpy since the strange incident with the removal of her bedding the other night.

"Can't you hear that?" Lizzy frowned at the others, "somebody is singing?"

They all went quiet and still, listening out. There was a light melody filling the air around them – an old sounding melody and they looked about unable to place where the singing was coming from.

Emma shrugged, "It'll be one of the other drama teams practicing their music." All the girls seemed satisfied with this justification, with the exception of Lizzy, who continued to stare off down the corridor, unnerved. Emma gave her a nudge.

"I don't like it either Lizzy, there are some weird things going on, I feel like a bag of nerves, C' mon," Emma encouraged, "let's go tell Mrs Stevens how awesome our play is going to be!"

Lizzy managed a half-smile at her best friend and Rosie took this as her cue to knock on the door.

"Enter!" Mrs Stevens called, and Rosie pushed on the old heavy wood door as she turned the steel doorknob.

"Ah Team Rosie! Yes – do come in and make yourselves comfortable!" Mrs Stevens gestured around her at various seats. Rosie took the tall stool seated next to Mrs Stevens, Emma slouched comfortably into an armchair, Dawn sat on the hard chair opposite the huge desk and Lizzy perched herself upon the wooden ledge of panelling that bordered the room. The room smelt strongly of roses and Lizzy found herself looking around the room to see where they were displayed – finding it odd as the scents usually distributed around the school at this time of year consisted of fir tree, cinnamon, chocolate, oranges, cloves, gingerbread baking and hot roast dinners. If Mrs Stevens had roses, they must have been bought for her in an unseasonal bouquet – but Lizzy couldn't see any and clocked into the conversation as Mrs Stevens was asking Emma and Rosie if the library was back to its ordered state.

"Yes" Emma smiled, "strangely, it did it all by itself." Emma had a smirk on her face which showed she knew Mrs Stevens had played a joke on them. Then Rosie chipped in "You really had us confused there Mrs Stevens; we spent hours talking about how it could have happened," she laughed. But Mrs Stevens wasn't laughing; in fact, she looked quite confused herself. "What are you talking about? I hope Mrs Winter didn't put them all back herself before you got there. I told you to get there early."

"We were there when she opened the library door at 8.30am, the books were all fine, on the shelves where they should be." Dawn said.

"Enough now girls, I don't care who put them all back, but I hope you have learned your lesson."

Emma protested "But Mrs Stevens, we...."

Dawn butted in, "We have most definitely learned our lesson and won't ever be going to the library out of normal hours again."

"Good to hear, so what is your play about?" Ms Steven said, obviously wishing to move on from the subject.

"It's a ghost story," Rosie declared proudly.

"A Christmas ghost story," Dawn clarified, and they all nodded.

"That sounds intriguing!!" Mrs Stevens clapped her hands together joyfully, "so, tell me, what was your chosen prop, to inspire a *ghost* story?"

The girls all exchanged glances.

"A board game!" Emma yelled, trying to answer before anybody else did.

"A *board game?*" Mrs Stevens frowned "...can you

elaborate on how a board game could be linked to a ghost story...?"

"We *could*, Mrs Stevens" began Emma, "but we'd really rather not."

"It's a surprise you see," Dawn added, "we really want the element of surprise to add to the suspense of the piece..."

Rosie nodded emphatically as Mrs Stevens looked to her to validate this approach.

Mrs Stevens sighed with resignation, "then I suppose there isn't much you can tell me about your project...?"

"Not really, Mrs Stevens," Emma smiled sweetly.

"Very well – off you go then and carry on devising. I'll look forward to witnessing the final result!" But as the girls went to stand, Mrs Stevens stopped them. "Before you go though, girls...nobody is in trouble, but -" the girls all stiffened, thinking she must have found the Ouija board and was playing them, testing to see if anybody would confess, "you do all know that it is prohibited to wear perfume during the weekdays?"

This stumped them.

"Perfume?" Dawn asked, perplexed.

They collectively breathed sighs of relief and visibly relaxed as they realised their plan hadn't been busted, but then exchanged looks of confusion at each other.

"I don't mind perfume and make-up on weekends or special events for the senior girls, as you know, but during school hours, we cannot permit it..." Mrs Stevens looked each one of them in the eye, silently requesting somebody own up.

"Is it the roses?" Lizzy suddenly queried. They all looked to her, realising that she had been totally quiet until now. Mrs Stevens took a long inhale to test the scent.

"Roses? Yes – I think it is the scent of rose -"

Lizzy nodded "I smelt it in here, Mrs Stevens. None of the girls smell of roses – I've been with them all day. I smelt roses the moment I entered your office. I've been looking around for your flowers."

"I have no flowers," Mrs Stevens replied, looking perplexed.

"I *can* smell roses," Dawn confirmed, as the others took deep breaths and nodded in agreement.

"But it's not any of you?" Mrs Stevens checked, looking around at them all.

They all shook their heads, looking entirely innocent.

"Hmph," Mrs Stevens shrugged, "no matter then. My apologies for the accusation."

"But you *do* smell roses, Miss?" Lizzy pressed.

"I do," Mrs Stevens nodded.

"Do you ever hear singing? Or humming? In the corridor particularly?" Lizzy asked, looking intently at her housemistress. The other three girls stared at her, mouths agog, wondering what she was doing.

Mrs Stevens laughed, "When the year sevens are practicing for choir in the hall, I certainly do hear a cacophony of singing!"

Lizzy remained serious, "But ever at night? Ever when there are no rehearsals, no Christmas plays being practiced?"

Rosie, Emma and Dawn looked between Mrs Stevens and Lizzy as if it were a tennis match. Mrs Steven's face twitched at a frown before settling into a much more solemn expression.

"Have you, by any chance, been reading up on the school's history as a basis for your ghost story, Lizzy?" Mrs Stevens tilted her head.

Lizzy shook her head no.

Mrs Stevens' eyes flitted between the four girls, as if deciding whether to share a fact that had come to mind, "They say that this corridor is haunted..."

All the girls tensed, with Rosie dramatically pulling in breath.

"They say -" Mrs Stevens continued, "that

humming and singing has been heard in this corridor for centuries when nobody is about and that there is a presence and particular chilliness by the doors in the dining room."

Rosie had her hand gripped to her chest; Emma and Dawn's mouths were wide open, and Lizzy went quite suddenly very pale.

"Personally, I think it's all total ridiculous," Mrs Stevens laughed, "but it might help you with some material for your play I suppose...which is the only reason I'm telling you. Please *do not* spread it around the junior girls, for heaven's sake – I'll have a house full of children refusing to sleep!"

"I've felt it," Lizzy nodded, "the coldness by the dining room door, even in the summer. And I've heard it – the singing and humming in the corridor" then she looked to her friends and half-whispered, "you've heard it too. You know you did."

Rosie looked directly to Mrs Stevens, "Are the other groups practicing their plays just now?"

"No - you're the last group I asked to see. As I have seen each group, I have released them for free period. So, you're free to go now too. Rehearsal is over for the day." Mrs Stevens smiled, closing the conversation.

The girls all exchanged knowing looks as they

thanked Mrs Stevens for her time and left her office, congregating in the corridor.

"Come on girls, this corridor gives me the creeps," Dawn instigated, and they all began to move back towards the main stairwell.

But as Lizzy passed her postal pigeon-hole, she noticed a solitary piece of folded paper in the cubby. She paused behind the group to slip her hand in and take it out, unfolding the paper with intrigue. As she flattened it out, she noted the only word written upon it; in black thick marker pen: *BETTY*.

Up ahead, Emma had started making silly 'woo-hoooo' ghost noises, in a bid to make Rosie and Dawn laugh out of the unnerved mood which had enveloped them – which they eventually ended up giggling along with her.

After a sharp intake of breath at reading the note, Lizzy recognised that her friends up ahead were laughing raucously down the corridor – this was clearly a big wind-up. Lizzy chased after her friends shouting, "Not funny guys; seriously, not funny," in a confident, jesting manner that she didn't feel.

The other three girls assumed Lizzy was reacting to Emma's silly ghost noises and didn't question her comment. Nobody mentioned the note. Lizzy screwed up the assumed joke-from-her-friends and tossed it into the plastic flip-bin halfway along the corridor. And there it sat. Disregarded by the group of young pretty girls. And the Author of the note did not like that at all.

CHAPTER 6
1875

Clara laid out on her bed, which was pure white bed linen – another bonus about living in her own flat at the top of the school was that she not only had her very own space, rent-free, but her linen was washed and pressed by the laundry staff, as often as she wished. If she had only been granted post of matron, along with the other girls on the Holly house staff, she should have hated sharing the flat below with one of the other matrons, dependent on who was on shift. Clara didn't like sharing. She had appealed to Alice's sentimental side when she interviewed for the job – emphasised how Alice's brother, Damien, God rest his soul, would never have wanted his wife to live in near-squalor, sharing rooms with virtual strangers.

She suggested that Damien's spirit would hardly be at rest at all with the idea that his wife now had to *work* and so it would lessen the blow at least if Clara could work closely with his sister, at the school and in the higher echelons of the staff so that she was well-treated and kept in a comfortable fashion.

The Headmistress, Mrs Alice Brown, had been more impressed by Rosemary Faulkner's proposal – a matron with twelve full years' experience at Meadowbank School; well-loved by children and staff alike. She believed in fairness, discipline and affection in well-balanced measures. She was efficient at her chores and studious in her interests such as needlework, flower arrangements, perfume-creation and music. Rosemary was the perfect candidate.

Except Clara had used that foolproof argument – Damien. Alice and Damien had always been very close as siblings and when he contracted Diphtheria, it seemed impossible the disease would snatch away such a strong, fit man. And when death came, Alice was not only unprepared but absolutely devastated. As Clara manipulated Alice's emotions regarding how Damien would feel about his wife's unfortunate situation, it seemed Alice had no choice – of course, she must grant Clara the post, in loving memory of her brother and the fact that it was what he would have wanted. Besides, Clara had spent six months as a governess for a rich family in London and then a further six months as a house matron at another school. Clara had not secured any references from either of those placements, even upon the Headmistresses' request, but Alice argued with herself that Clara was *family* and that was character reference enough.

And so it was that Clara found herself stretching out on the freshly starched bed linen of the top-floor flat, pondering what disgusting chores she might dish out to Rosemary Faulkner today to keep the woman in line. She despised the audacity of Rosemary – sticking her nose into situations where she wasn't wanted and making ludicrous accusations. George was the best thing to have happened to Clara in years and that loathsome Rosemary Faulkner was hell-bent on ruining it for her. Clara bet that Rosemary was bitter Clara had won the house-mistress job over her and just trying to make things difficult. It was very unfortunate that Rosemary had witnessed Clara sneaking George back out the dining room doors that night – if it hadn't been for that, Rosemary would have no ammunition to use against her.

As Clara thought about George, she couldn't help the smile that came across her face. He was tall, muscular and strong – totally different to Damien, who had been lean and sinewy. Damien had always sported a pale, clear complexion; almost feminine in his appearance, whereas George was tanned, weathered, rugged and a bit rough around the edges. In temperament too – Damien couldn't do enough for Clara; always buying her gifts, ensuring she was comfortable. Clara revelled in that of course, but it had also always struck her as quite pathetic and needy; Damien was desperate for her approval. George didn't need it – he had a wild confidence. He knew that he was attractive to most women he came across and not caring about it somehow enhanced his popularity. But he'd also come through a similar tragedy to Clara herself – George had told her, during one of their earliest chats, that he had lost his wife when she was pregnant with their child. A double tragedy in fact, having lost his wife and unborn child in one fell swoop. Clara and George had common ground here – they were both grieving, both loveless – both hoping to find solace elsewhere. Clara found that she didn't miss Damien anymore, since George had entered her office during her first week and her attention had shifted from the pity she consistently allowed herself to indulge in, to focus on how she could get that man to notice her. In the end, she hadn't needed to formulate a plan – he approached her and made quite obvious advances; making her laugh at his rather crude jokes – she hadn't laughed that way in a long time, if ever. Clara came to realise that it had not been Damien she had been missing – it had been the comfortable existence he had bestowed upon her. Now she had a highly masculine man, who wanted her hungrily and seemed never to be satiated. And a lovely space of her own that she didn't have to share. After two years of turbulence, things were starting to feel satisfactory again. When Damien's Diphtheria was worsening, he had warned her that there were not any funds of great extravagance to come to her when he passed – which had shocked her.

"Why?" she had asked, "you have always treated me to such expensive gifts and entertained me with the high life…"

Damien laughed weakly and cocked his eyebrow with irony, "That, my love, is why we have not much left…" It turned out he had been indulging Clara for her every want and need and earning well, but never with much money left at the end of the month. Now he was no longer working, that money had disappeared extremely quickly. Clara descended into a pit of fear, imagining a factory-line job, sweaty, foul fug of chimney smoke engulfing her every day, or worse, having to prostitute herself to earn her bread. She did not spend much time around Damien in his last few days, resenting his impulsive spending that had led her into this potentially destitute future. When he did eventually die, Clara ingratiated herself with Damien's elder sister, Alice, who she knew was successful and wealthy and would not allow her sister-in-law to fall into a life of poverty – so long as she was a close friend. Alice and Clara had not been very much involved in each other's lives while Damien was alive, but now Clara ensured she became a confidante to Alice whilst she grieved – Clara was around for every boring hour of Alice's tears and tedious retelling of nostalgic stories of her brother from her childhood. Clara cried in the right places and laughed with her new-found best friend, until Alice entirely trusted her and told her that she understood why her brother had chosen such a generous-spirited, kind and loyal woman as his wife. Clara nodded proudly as Alice's back turned – she felt satisfied that she had inserted herself so importantly into Alice's life that there was no way she would stand by as her sister-in-law struggled financially. Essentially, she had rescued herself. Clara had managed to do this before, with Damien – and she would go on doing this however she needed to, in order to keep her head above water. She had learnt that nobody else was going to consistently do this for her.

But George Stone was something else. He was not going to provide for her – his lower status would be frowned upon in the high society that she now mingled with. He was unlikely to protect her – in fact sometimes in their throes of passion, it felt as though he was capable of the opposite; he would hold his hands at her throat and release a guttural groan. He felt dangerous and this attracted Clara in a way she had never felt for anybody ever before. It was an animalistic attraction, something so primal and so far from domesticity or security that it enticed Clara until she felt addicted. George Stone was just the man she needed in her life.

If Rosemary Faulkner thought she was going to stand in Clara's way of this new, exciting gratification, she could forget it.

CLARA HADN'T SLEPT WELL, despite having no nocturnal visits – even on nights when George threw stones at her window quite late and she hurried down the twisty staircases to let him in at the dining room doors, full of lust and unravelling each other as they backed down the corridor wrapped in each other, moving towards the little sofa in her office – she would sleep well afterwards. It was as if he released something in her that helped her to rest.

Yesterday, he had been in an understandably bad mood after the unfortunate mishap with that distracting girl Betty Grainger – added to this the probable knowing that the nuisance Rosemary Faulkner would no doubt have reported him. So, Clara had known better than to approach him and ask if he wanted to meet that night – she had come to recognise that thundercloud over his head and know when to give him a wide berth. She had wondered if the now-familiar tap of stones at her window might arrive later in the night and anticipating them kept her awake. Then when no night-caller came, the disappointment kept her awake even longer. She yawned as she crossed the lawn this morning, under the guise of requesting George prune the thorny branches that were beginning to impede the footpath that ran alongside the rose-garden. She knocked on his potting shed door and as she heard his footsteps approach, she pushed out her bosom and stood straighter, preparing a sweet smile for him.

He opened the door gruffly – still in an apparent bad mood. As he saw who was standing at his door, a lop-sided grin graced his browning teeth on one side, and he raised an eyebrow in a way that half made Clara's heart skip and half made her wonder if - as his thick, dark hair greyed further - he might just look a bit depraved. She shook her head, flicking her fringe to the side and the ugly thought away with it.

"Good morning, George," she smiled flirtatiously.

"To what do I owe this pleasure?" he growled.

"I've come to ask you to prune back the thorny branches on the rose-garden border, please," she licked her lips in a suggestive fashion.

George grinned wider now and she could smell a foulness on his breath, then a thought seemed to steal away his happy thoughts.

"That woman – she wants some roses," he garbled.

Clara had become accustomed to the way George would sometimes just blurt out his thoughts, entirely out of context.

"Pardon?" she queried.

"Rosemary. *That* woman," he identified with disgust.

"Rosemary?"

"She wants roses – for a perfume or something..." he clarified.

"Ah yes..." Clara's thoughts seemed to wander momentarily.

"Shall I throw them all on the compost? Pretend I forgot?" George slung his bulky arms across his chest and leaned on the wooden doorframe.

Clara thought for a moment, "No...no, give her the roses. Lots of them."

George frowned, until a devious thought occurred to him, "Ah! Mix in a posy of deadly nightshade?" he cackled, which Clara instantly thought wasn't a fitting sound from this bulk of a man.

"No," she snapped at him for not understanding her train of thought, "give her the roses generously. She mistrusts you. Give her a reason to question her harsh judgement. Show her how nice you are."

George laughed gutturally now – a hearty chuckle that was much more appropriate for his substantial physical presence.

"I'm not nice..." he leaned into Clara as he whispered it. She didn't take it in the playful way he meant it, but instead cocked an eyebrow at him and warned, "well, *play* nice. We need to keep her onside."

He leaned back, reprimanded but not happy about it. Clara instantly wanted to salvage the cheerful mood and whispered, with levity, "you didn't come for me last night..."

George shrugged and looked over her head. Clara turned in the direction of his eyeline and saw a gaggle of girls leaving the dining room, crossing the lawn towards the tennis courts, in their feminine white sporting outfits. His eyes sparkled as he watched them.

"Maybe later, my love," he purred, still not taking his eyes off the group of girls.

"But now," George looked back at Clara, as if remembering she was there, "to the rose garden!"

Clara smiled briefly and nodded just once, before turning to cross the lawn back to her office via the dining room doors. As she walked, poised and feeling watched, she tried not to let her mind torture her with the fact that the rose garden was right next to the tennis courts...

. . .

Clara decided to get on with the dormitory inspections as this was the first duty on her list following breakfast service. She gathered her clipboard and lead pencil for her office and started to make her way down the corridor. She noted on her way that all of the postal pigeonholes had been emptied and delivered, and she nodded in satisfaction. But then noticed one piece of white paper sitting in her own pigeon-hole at the end of the rows, at the top. She reached curiously up to it and unfolded it, noting how thin the paper was – it was the sort that was made very cheaply; there was a tear down one side of it where it had been pulled from a notebook. The scrawl was obviously attempting to be ornate but was written in an untrained hand and it read '*I missed you last night. You are the only woman in my life. G.*' Clara looked nervously about herself to check nobody had seen, then quickly folded the note and held it to her chest with a deep breath and a triumphant smile. From a man like George, this was as good as an 'I love you'. He wasn't the sort to go all soppy on her and this was the first romantic gesture he had made. Clara deposited the note inside the pocket of her apron and walked down the corridor with more of a spring in her step.

. . .

It was with some trepidation that Clara inspected the senior girl's dormitory – if she found any further contraband, she felt sure that Rosemary would be back on her mission to frame George as the perpetrator. She took particular care in Betty's dormitory – searching under her well-made bed and throughout her section of the wardrobe. Betty's clothes had a soft, floral scent about them – she was just so young and pretty, damn her. Educated, with her life ahead of her and her long red hair drew the eyes of so many potential suitors. Clara felt sick with envy and felt an instinct to spit. She held herself back from doing so, swallowed hard and left the room in a hurry, almost angry that she could find no reason to expel the girl and remove this pretty distraction.

After a morning of checks – for the boarding house was vast and some of the girls a lot messier than others – Clara had confiscated a book that she considered to be too adult in nature for a child's consumption. She had noted the offenders' names down and would speak with them individually later that day. As she descended the staircase, planning on asking the pantry staff to prepare her a pot of tea, she saw Rosemary walking up the stairs towards her flat – her arms were bundled with pink roses, and she couldn't help the smile that played upon her lips. Clara feigned innocence, "What pretty roses you have there, Rosemary!"

Rosemary stopped and her expression of shock was impossible to disguise, then she composed herself and forced a smile at Clara, "Yes – they're beautiful, aren't they?"

"Are you courting somebody from the village?" Clara cocked an eyebrow.

"Oh no -" Rosemary blushed at the suggestion, "I'm merely collecting them for making perfume..."

"Ah. That must be expensive – to buy all of those roses for the ingredients?" Clara would *make* Rosemary say it.

"No – actually, George gave these to me..." Rosemary looked at the floor and then up at Clara through her eyelashes.

"George Stone, the Gardener?" Clara pretended he was someone who spent little time on her mind, "what a kind and generous thing to do!" Clara let it hang there a moment.

Rosemary swallowed hard, consulting the floor "...yes..." she said quietly, reluctantly.

"Such a thoughtful fellow..." Clara threw out the

comment as she passed Rosemary on the stairs and continued her way to the pantry, noting the stillness of Rosemary before she continued on her way up the stairs. *Good*, Clara thought, *she won't be any more trouble. She owes George now and she's realising the error of her judgement.* Clara popped her head into the pantry to request a pot of tea be brought to her office and thought for a moment she saw a roll of eyes upon the staff member who then prepared a smile for her and nodded. Clara saw sunshine through the small corridor window that looked out upon the lawn and decided to take in a few moments of fresh air whilst her tea was being prepared. She opened the creaking dining room doors – which she cursed for the way their metal always caught on the gravel path in the ugliest noise – and stepped out on to the lawn. She looked across at the potting shed but saw no activity there. She hoped to commend George on his early-morning gesture with the rose and impress upon him just how helpful this will have been. But then she wondered if this was one of the days George might be taking some leave – she knew there were days he went back to the house he used to share with his poor wife in the village. She pondered with sadness if this was a place he went to for grieving his loss;

the one place he could allow his emotions to be expressed more crudely. The thought of that great hulk of masculinity crying made her feel weak with pity for him – it made her want to embrace him. Perhaps one day she would feel that she could ask him about his old family home in the village; perhaps one day they might share a day of leave, and he could take her there to visit? She became aware that as these thoughts had monopolised her mind, she had been ambling across the lawn towards the shed and was now standing half-way between the main boarding house and George's shed. She realised with a start that this wouldn't do at all to be seen daydreaming at the handsome Gardener's abode. With a sobering shake of her head, she turned abruptly back towards the boarding house and saw – up at a second-storey window - the bulky mass of a man that was unmistakenly George Stone. At first, Clara's mind could not compute why he was up on a ladder, peering into a window. Then, with horror, she counted along the windows from the core staircase glazing – which was distinguishable by its patterns of geometric rhombus shapes. She counted along three dormitory-style windows, one frosted glazing for the bathroom and then the next window – the one which George was peering into –

was undoubtedly the changing rooms. Then, Clara came to the disastrous understanding that the girls should just have finished their tennis lessons for the morning and would now be changing into their uniforms for lunchtime and afternoon lessons...

Clara considered shouting out – to give him the chance to justify his actions – there must be a reasonable explanation for him being at that window. But what if her shout alerted other people as to what it seemed he was doing? Her instinct to protect him above all else won her over and so she knew she needed to disappear quickly, before she was seen by anybody else to be ignoring the situation and before he turned to see her and possibly fell off the ladder in surprise. She carried her skirts in one hand and practically ran to the dining room doors, flying in past the hot food counter smelling of stewed cabbage and roasted beef and flung herself into her office. She was relieved to see that the pantry staff had delivered her pot of tea – she poured herself a cup of black tea, added two sugarlumps for the shock and began to drink it as she sank into her chair, welcoming the intense heat that scorched her tongue as she drank it down. Welcoming the pain of the hot liquid; welcoming any distraction from what she had just seen.

. . .

Clara had to wait until George came to visit her that evening before she could speak to him about the ladder incident – and that was if she even chose to. She knew that she had been distracted during her work – forgetting to lay out glasses for the student's' water jugs during dinner service; neglecting to speak to the offending girls about the various contraband found in their dormitories. She was short with people in her interactions too – Rosemary had approached in a sunny mood, asking if Clara would like sample of rose perfume once she had produced it. Clara snapped that she *hated* the smell of roses. In hindsight, perhaps she should have thanked her and accepted, to keep her sweet, but her head was too busy with this terrible dilemma for her to retain any patience for anybody else.

She spent the afternoon ricocheting from one decision to another – in the first instance, she knew she needed to ask George what he was doing up on a ladder at the changing room window – he likely had a reasonable justification and once she knew what that was, she would be able to move forward in confidence, enjoying their romance as she had been before Rosemary had planted these unnerving ideas in her head. Then, she countered that really, did she actually need to know? George was a valuable addition to her life – what if, by asking, she proved a distrust of his character which he just couldn't forgive? If – as she assumed – he had a perfectly pedestrian explanation, he would be well within his rights to be very angry at the hidden accusation behind her questioning. She should stay quiet.

But if she never asked, that concern would always be in the back of her mind, taunting her, standing in the way of their relationship....

The indecision was infuriating. Usually, Clara was so forthright and decisive – this was an unfamiliar experience to her and one which she was not enjoying in the least.

Eventually, by the time she was sitting in the dark of the dining room, waiting to see George's tall silhouette approach the dining room doors, she had worked herself up into such a state that it would be impossible to act relaxed and unaffected in front of him, so that essentially made the decision for her.

Clara cringed as she pushed open the noisy door, hoping she didn't attract unwanted attention. George lunged forward to embrace her and his eager lips even met hers briefly before she had the chance to hold up her palms in defence. His face took on an ugly displeasure as he registered her reluctance and Clara took a step back, whispering, "I just need to talk to you first…come into my office…" she still took his hand, in a gesture to show that her query was not intended in a negative manner; that it was merely something she wanted to discuss.

They disappeared through the doorway of her office and George closed it behind them as she bent to light the lantern with a candle. He let out his usual "ooof" sound as he lowered himself onto her sofa-bed. Then he spread his legs wide apart – it always shocked Clara how the man managed to take up the majority of the room when he relaxed. She turned, in the lamplight and smiled, to soften the blow of what she was about to ask.

"Thank you for the note you left me this morning," Clara whispered, acting cute. Then she sidled over to him.

"I just…" she began and then realised that in her indecision of *whether* to say anything, she had at no point decided *what* to say.

George let out an impatient sigh.

"I saw you earlier on the ladder," Clara blurted out. That was all she needed to say – his reaction would tell her the truth of the story.

George's mouth fell open and he nodded, just once.

"What – what were you doing up there?" Clara fidgeted at her skirts, afraid of what he might say.

"Cleaning the gutters," George stated.

Clara looked at him intently "...the gutters? You were?"

"They get leaves and moss in them, don't they?" George grunted.

"I suppose they must, yes. But – but you didn't have a bucket to collect the debris from the gutters?" Clara prompted further.

George furrowed his brow at her, "It's easier to throw the stuff down from the gutters, then collect it when it's on the ground. I keep my balance better – have you ever tried climbing a ladder with a bucket in one hand?"

Clara laughed a little, "I've never climbed a ladder..."

"Well, take it from me; climb with both hands," George confirmed.

Clara smiled at him, feeling a relief after a day of worrying. His explanation *did* make sense. And he had justified it so calmly.

Clara came to sit upon his lap, as she had done so many times recently on this very sofa-bed. His broad legs made her feel dainty and doll-like. She realised how like a child her small frame looked next to his. She smoothed her small, delicate hands over his large face and was about to lean in to kiss him, when this time it was George who pulled back and frowned in her face, "What did you think I was doing on the ladder?"

Clara breathed quickly inwards, "Oh, I only meant to warn you...I'm sure you didn't know – but the window you were at looks in upon the girls' changing rooms. And I do believe the timing of your gutter-cleaning coincided with the end of their tennis lessons. I was only worried that if the girls saw you there, they might jump to more terrible conclusions, in the same way that awful Betty Grainger did the other day."

George held her gaze for a moment longer than necessary and in that beat, she wondered if he believed her – that she had been concerned only for *him*. And if he didn't believe her, how might he react?

Then he smiled at her, in that crooked way he did and pulled her in closer to him "*That*. Would have been terrible."

Then he kissed her, and she allowed herself to believe he was an honest man.

CHAPTER 7
PRESENT DAY

"Right! Girls, it is written!" Rosie announced, clasping her hands together at her chest, "I'll read the entire play to you all this evening after dinner," she slotted herself into her chair in front of the lasagne and garlic bread that awaited her, and which the other girls were already half-way through.

"Where will we read it?" Lizzy asked, swallowing a mouthful of pasta sheet and bechamel.

"In our dorm, of course," Emma shrugged.

"Ah – could we not?" Lizzy fidgeted. The night of the duvet-removal was still raw in her mind and the others respected her discomfort.

"Down here, then," Dawn suggested, "in the

dining room; I can ask Mrs Stevens if it's okay to use the space."

"Oooh, we can make it even more spooky by keeping the lights off and using our flashlights!" Emma giggled, always loving to embellish experiences with extra sensory garnish. The other girls laughed at her enthusiasm.

It was around eight PM when the four girls made their way down the stairs, with Rosie clutching the manuscript territorially.

"Where did you say you went last night?" Lizzy asked Rosie.

"I didn't say," Rosie responded haughtily, and the other girls exchanged sarcastic glances.

"Did your Mum and Dad come to take you out?" Dawn hazarded a guess.

"Nope," Rosie closed the conversation.

Lizzy *really* wanted to know. Rosie had sloped off around dinnertime, citing that she would have no time to write the play that evening, due to *'prior plans'*. The girls had asked her where she was going but she had been so mysterious, then changed herself into jeans and a smart off-the-shoulder dusky pink jumper that complimented her blonde hair and been called by matron that her lift had arrived. And she hadn't returned until about ten PM. The secrecy infuriated Lizzy – simply because the four of them rarely held secrets from each other and Lizzy was also worried that there might be some elaborate plan they were all plotting against her in relation to the play and how much the other evening had scared her. So, Lizzy had done something she'd never done before – something she felt very guilty about now. After dinner this evening, as Dawn and Emma went to ask Mrs Stevens if they could use the dining room for the play reading and whilst Rosie showered, Lizzy had sneakily taken Rosie's diary from her bedside table drawer and opened it at the most recent entry. As she did it, she felt watched – she knew this was just the guilt and the fact she knew what she was doing was immoral, but she had to keep looking over at the door, to check nobody could see her. Only the draw of the watchful feeling wasn't over at the door – it was from the window. She tried to ignore it and hungrily read the diary entry from yesterday. Oh!

Mum and Dad picked me up to join them for a drink, meeting their friend who is a university lecturer in medicine at Oxford. They seem to think he has some sway with uni scholarships if he's particularly impressed with the candidate. I tried hard enough to be impressive so that Mum and Dad wouldn't be embarrassed in front of their friend for wasting his time, but also made it very clear through my conversation that I'm hoping to study drama and theatre and not follow Mum and Dad in their footsteps as doctors. I nearly told Dawn about it, because she knows I struggle with their constant pushing for me to go into Medicine professionally. But I want my friends to take my ambitions seriously – especially as I'm currently writing our end-of-term play and taking the lead part in it. If they know that I'm discussing potential university medical courses, they will stop believing in me and the likelihood that I could *actually make it in acting one day. So I'll stay quiet – it won't come to anything anyway. Rather they guess that I was at an audition – that would have been way cooler!*

As Lizzy consumed that last sentence, a shadow moved over her very suddenly. In the instant in which her eyeline moved to the window, the lamplight from outside was in full beam once again. It was as if something had momentarily blocked the light from the lamppost. Lizzy stared at the window, almost daring it to go dark again, although her heart was hammering in her chest. Then she snapped out of her reverie, realising that she was sitting with

Rosie's diary open on her lap. She quickly closed it and replaced it as she had found it.

Now, as they all headed down the dark corridor with their torches switched on, she felt terrible for snooping – especially when it had turned out it had absolutely nothing to do with her or with the spooky business of the play. She'd asked Rosie again in the hope of reinforcing her innocence, but Rosie was steadfast.

All of a sudden, she could smell roses again; it was strong, really potent- as if somebody had just sprayed perfume under her nose. The others seemed to smell it too and all came to a standstill next to the postal pigeon-holes, just looking at each other in silence and breathing in the scent. Then came the very distant sweet melody of a female voice humming…it was further down the corridor towards the dining room. Their eyes sparkled and blazed in a combined mixture of disbelief and horror. Emma took Lizzy's hand and started creeping her further down the corridor towards the dining room – Rosie clutched onto Lizzy and grabbed Dawn to follow and the four of them tiptoed into the darkness in a shaky line. Suddenly, the door to Mrs Steven's office flew open.

"Boo!" she yelled and then laughed in a good-humoured way as they jumped. She switched on her office light, causing them all to blink and rub at their eyes.

"Here to read your spooooooooky play?" Mrs Stevens laughed again. "I'm heading upstairs now girls, so just make sure you turn out the lights before you go up to bed. Security will check the perimeter later on this evening, but they don't come inside, so be sure to do that for me, okay?"

The girls nodded and replied with 'good nights' as Mrs Stevens turned off her office light once more and strode away from them down the corridor.

"Was it her who was humming?" Dawn asked the others.

"Of course it was!" Emma laughed, "she was winding us up!"

"Did she also buy some rose perfume...?" Lizzy murmured partially to herself as she followed the group descending on the dining room.

"Let's leave the lights off!" Emma boomed as they entered the dining room.

Lizzy wanted to protest but didn't want to stand out as the nervous one, in case the girls decided to play any more tricks on her like the postal pigeon-hole prank the other day – anyway, she countered, she could rely on Rosie to be the nervous one insisting the lights went on.

"Good idea!" Rosie piped up, "if I read the play by torchlight, it will really emphasise the overall atmosphere of the intended edginess..."

"But Rosie," Lizzy protested, "what happened to you being scared of your own shadow?"

Rosie seemed offended by this, whipping her long blonde ponytail around to look at Lizzy.

"I hate the Ouija board. I'm *worried about* the Ouija board. Tonight, I'm just reading you the play I invented in my own head...well, I mean, I used some of the names you guys managed to research but -"

"You did?!" Dawn was excited at the prospect of having added something valuable to the creation of the script.

Rosie nodded proudly "I did – but my point is that I'm not afraid of something I made up in my own head."

Lizzy shrugged. She guessed they were doing this thing in the dark.

They all sat in a circle, cross-legged on the floor, each holding a torch in the dark. There was a sense of anticipation in the air, as Rosie pointed her torch at the manuscript and cleared her throat.

"*Lights come up on the stage, with a spotlight on*

the under-stage door, which is open. Four girls emerge from the door under the stage, one at a time. The very last one is holding a Ouija board. They stand staring at the audience for a moment, looking worried, questioning – then there is a sudden shrill scream from somewhere offstage and all the lights switch suddenly to black..."

Dawn and Emma giggle with nervous excitement, "oh my god, Rosie – that's a really creepy start!" Emma shuffles about, causing her flashlight to roam around the corners of the dark dining hall.

"It's deliciously dramatic!" Dawn compliments, trying to use descriptive language that Rosie would approve of. Rosie smiled looking proud.

"*Scene one...*" Rosie begins but is interrupted by Emma.

"Don't you mean scene two?"

"No – that initial montage was more of a prologue," Rosie explained, keen to proceed.

"You know Emma, like in English lit when -" Lizzy began to illustrate but she was interrupted by all the three other girls shrieking looking towards the dining room doors. Lizzy turned swiftly to see the silhouette of a large, tall man outside through the glass of dining room doors – he was standing with his face close to the glass as if he was peering in at them, but any details of his features were shrouded in shadow.

"Shit!" Dawn scrambled away from her position which was closest to the door.

"Who the hell is that!?" Emma yelled.

"Security, surely?" Lizzy proposed, sounding a hell of a lot calmer than she felt, "didn't Mrs Stevens say Security would be checking the perimeter?"

The girls all looked at her, wild eyes looking deranged in their torchlights, then as they all looked back to the doors again, the silhouette had gone.

"He's gone anyway," Rosie breathed, "haha – *we* probably scared *him*, with our flashlights – he probably thought the place was being burgled!"

The girls breathed easy for a moment as they realised the probable truth in what Rosie was saying. Lizzy kept an eye on the lawn between the doors and the old potting shed as Rosie continued with the story.

"*Lights up on a dormitory,*"

"Will we be building a set?" Dawn asked.

"I think we'll keep it pretty basic," Rosie replied, "some props suggestive of where the characters are, but not an actual *set*."

Dawn nodded, satisfied with this approach.

"So, the thing to remember guys, is this is a *play*

within a play. Shakespeare used this format a lot, so it's a winning strategy for getting a story across" Rosie was in her element – coming alive as she spoke about her favourite thing.

"So, are we basically telling the story of what has happened to us, but through a play so nobody knows it's real?" Dawn asked.

Rosie squished her nose up, "sort of, to begin with. Then it takes a really wild turn and there's a great scary twist for the audience."

There were various 'oohs' from Emma and Dawn, but this wasn't Lizzy's area of expertise, and she was consumed by a strange feeling.

"Is anybody else feeling really cold?" Lizzy asked.

"Well, it is Decem -" but before Emma could finish her sentence, there was a loud rattling, shaking of the dining room doors as if somebody was trying to get in. This time all the girls screamed, jumped to their feet and ran to the back of the dining room, the furthest point away from the garden doors. The strangest thing was that they were clearly hearing and seeing the doors protest against somebody outside shaking them violently, but they could see nobody outside. The noise lasted for about five seconds and then fell totally silent. All that could be heard was the girls cowering, heavy breaths as they huddled together, watching the door.

"Was it the security guard?" Dawn asked.

"Didn't Mrs Stevens say *they don't come in*?" Rosie reminded her.

"Perhaps because he saw the light from our torches?" offered Emma.

"Guys," whispered Lizzy, "did you *see* anyone at the door?"

The girls all looked around at each other, unwilling to admit what they all knew.

"There was nobody there," Lizzy confirmed, "none that we could *see* anyway…"

"Okay, I think I'm done for tonight," Rosie shook her head and started for the corridor – the others needed no further encouragement to join her.

"We'll continue the play tomorrow when it's *daylight*," Rosie continued as they pushed on together through the corridor, their flashlights dancing, illuminating dark corners.

Lizzy raised her flashlight to the pigeon-holes out of habit, always eager to see if anybody had written to her from home. She noticed there *was* a slip of white paper in the cubby; she pulled it out discreetly as she passed and – in the darkness where none of the other girls could see it – unfolded it in her hand, then passed a quick beam of light from her torch over it, fast enough to see the scrawled letters *BETTY YOU ARE MINE*. Lizzy was about to yell at her friends – but then reasoned that one of them would have slipped it into the pigeon-hole on their way down to the dining room earlier, before the rose scent, the humming, the silhouette and the rattling door; she felt certain that given the current turn of events, they wouldn't have been so insensitive. It wasn't worth calling them out on a prank now, when there were more frightening things to consider. Lizzy balled the note up in a clenched fist and stuck it deep into the pocket of her jogging bottoms. She was pretty sure the pranks from her friends would stop now that things had gotten so real.

"We can't rehearse in the recreation hall with all the other groups – they'll hear what our play is about," Dawn advised her friends the following morning.

"And worse still, they'll see our prop!" Emma warned.

Lizzy and Rosie considered this for a moment.

"I'm not sure I want to rehearse in the dining room after last night..." Lizzy volunteered.

"They'd be setting for lunch anyway; they wouldn't allow it," Rosie stated, "we could start reading it in the downstairs cloakroom – we wouldn't need permission for that. I'll just let the matrons know that's where we'll be practicing."

The girls all agreed upon this rather spacious area; it was where the outdoor coats and bags would hang upon pegs, and shoes would reside upon benches around the perimeter of the room, and in the centre was a large open space. It lent itself perfectly as rehearsal space and was located in between the Matron's Office and the Post Room, just along from the Recreation Hall where the other groups would be rehearsing, so it would be private, but they wouldn't be too out of touch if anybody needed them.

Rosie pointed to the space under Lizzy's bed, "Let's get the prop out then."

Everybody stilled.

"Do we need to use it *today?*" Lizzy asked.

"We really do. Last night was just going to be a read-through – I know that kind of fell apart," Rosie rolled her eyes as she said it, "but I've decided the most productive way to move forward is to jump straight into it – dialogue and action all at once, so that you all gain a deeper understanding of the essence of the play."

Emma bit her lip, trying not to laugh at Rosie's flamboyance.

"But you were the one who was the most reluctant for us to use the Ouija board at all, Hermione..." Dawn reminded Rosie.

"I was. And if I could turn back the clock, we'd be choosing a plastic Christmas tree and making a play up about *that*, but we are where we are and now that the play is written, we really ought to just get on with it. So, let's pull out the bloody Ouija board and get it down to the cloakroom without anyone seeing it."

Dawn and Emma shared a cautious glance – they were the only ones who had actually experienced *contacting* somebody on that board and they weren't feeling too keen about re-living the moment.

"Come on guys," Rosie encouraged, "remember, we're not actually *using* the board – we're only *acting* using the board."

With this, it seemed decided, and Lizzy gestured to her bed for any volunteers to fetch it. Emma stepped forward and slid the board from under the bed. Dawn retrieved a plastic bag from the wardrobe and wrapped the board in it, then they all made their way covertly downstairs towards the cloakroom.

Rosie set a little table in the middle of the cloakroom, and Emma placed the Ouija board upon it. Lizzy had reluctantly bought along her water glass from the dorm room and set it next to the board.

"So, we covered the prologue last night," Rosie uttered, "scene one is just some dialogue where the four characters google how to use a Ouija board – I know you've all read the dialogue for that bit so let's proceed with scene two -now the lights come up on the four of us crouched around this table and we're already engaged in the Ouija board experience - the scene starts at the moment the glass starts to move. So, it's straight into the action."

"How about I hold up the script for you all to read as we go?" Lizzy offered, reluctant to participate with the board.

"Good idea," Rosie nodded, handing it over, "the rest of us have our fingers on the glass like this." Rosie demonstrated and Emma and Dawn copied her.

Lizzy took a deep breath, "Okay, so it says here,

the glass begins to move and Character One spells out the letters as they come."

"I'm Character One," Rosie announced.

"Of course you are," Emma chortled. The girls all giggled, but there was a thin veil of nervousness behind it.

"So, as it moves," Lizzy continued, "the word it spells out is *ROSEMARY.*"

The girls started to push the glass towards 'R', but a strangeness fell over their faces as it landed instead on 'B'.

"No, it's supposed to be R for Rosemary," Rosie told Emma and Dawn looking at them accusingly.

"That's where I was pushing it." Emma laughed nervously.

"Me too!" Dawn found Emma's laughter contagious.

The glass moved again to 'E', then 'T, then moved across the board and back again to 'T' in quick succession.

"Which one of you is doing this?" screeched Rosie.

"Honestly I'm not!" Dawn squealed excitedly.

"No, me either..." Emma added, giggling.

Lizzy watched as the glass flew across the board,

noting which letters it paused at and then translated:

"Betty," she stated, stone-cold, "you guys spelled Betty instead of Rosemary." She looked up at them petulantly, "this really isn't funny".

"Could we please follow the script, girls?" Rosie rolled her eyes at their childishness. Emma and Dawn looked aghast at the accusation but couldn't stop laughing.

"Let's pretend you spelled Rosemary with it and carry on" Lizzy instructed, "the next part it is to spell - and Character One continues to read out the letters as they are spelled out – is HELLO. So, off you go... H..."

The girls began once again to push the glass towards H, but it went instead to I, then W, A, N, T...

"I WANT? What the hell are you two doing?" Rosie yelled at Dawn and Emma, "we're never going to get this play rehearsed all the way through today if you keep arsing around."

But the glass kept moving and Lizzy watched where it went. Y.O.U.

"I want you," Lizzy interpreted.

Then it flew to one more letter and stayed there. B.

"B," Lizzy whispered, and the other girls all looked over at her.

"Is this some kind of wind-up, you guys?"

Emma and Dawn were laughing at their protestations, and Lizzy knew she wouldn't get the truth out of them.

"Rosie," Lizzy appealed, "can you literally feel them pushing the glass?"

"Well, no..." Rosie acquiesced.

Lizzy placed the script on one of the benches, stood up and went to leave.

"I need a minute..."

The other girls chorused to encourage her to stay, but they were getting on her nerves, and she'd really thought after last night's scare they might lay off taunting her a bit. Lizzy stepped out into the corridor, where she was instantly hit by a wave of rose scent. She stopped and closed her eyes. Was this what going mad felt like? She reasoned with herself that somebody who worked in a room off this corridor- perhaps the offices, post-room, laundry or kitchens wore their perfume floral and strong.

Lizzy took a little stroll along the corridor to calm herself down – but was struck with dread as she noticed, in among the empty pigeon-holes, hers had a note – a simple piece of white paper. She grabbed it angrily, tore it open to read the words MEET ME AT THE POTTING SHED TONIGHT AT 8PM.

That was it. Lizzy turned on her heel and pushed her way back into the cloakroom.

"This," she held up the note to her friends, "is absolutely NOT funny. I've been trying to laugh along with you all and your immature antics, but seriously I've had enough of this now. No more fake Ouija board messages – no more notes in my pigeon-hole. This has got to stop. Okay?"

Her three friends were no longer laughing, but staring at her, incredulous. Lizzy rarely got snappy at anybody.

"What does it say?" Emma reached out her hand to the note.

Lizzy shoved it towards Emma, who read it aloud to the others,

"MEET ME AT THE POTTING SHED TONIGHT AT 8PM" then they all looked back at Lizzy, innocently.

"Who's it from?" Emma asked, wide-eyed.

Lizzy lifted one shoulder to her ear and raised her eyebrows at them all, "you!? All of you –

pranking me, pretending the 'ghost' is trying to talk to 'B'…"

"Oh!" Emma suddenly realised and turned to the others as in explanation, "because the 'B' could stand for 'Lizzy…'?"

This struck Lizzy as strange – if this thought hadn't previously occurred to Emma, had she just been playing along with Rosie and Dawn's plan?

"It's not from us," Rosie stated, "you know I'm as freaked out by this whole thing as you are. I wouldn't do that."

Dawn, then? It seemed unlikely – Dawn was always up for a joke but was usually a follower more than a leader.

"So, if it's not you guys, who do you expect me to believe this note is from?" Lizzy cocked her head, with hands on her hips.

The girls all looked at each other, unsure how to respond.

"Maybe we just need to go to the potting shed at 8pm?" Emma suggested with a mischievous grin.

"IN THEORY, to do this properly, we should really be down at the potting shed in the garden" Emma stated, whispering to the others in the darkness of the changing room window.

"We can see everything clearly here from the second-floor window" Rosie justified, "the garden is well-lit by the solar lights – if anybody turns up to meet you Lizzy, we'll see who it is without being in any danger at all."

Lizzy nodded, unable to take her eyes from the potting shed door.

"It's 7.59pm," Dawn advised, and they all drew a breath, watching intently.

Suddenly, they heard the screeching of the dining room doors opening and Rosie grabbed Lizzy's hand as they saw the movement of a shadow on the dark path approaching the potting shed.

"Oh my God," Dawn squealed, "thank God we stayed up here – they're carrying a weapon!!"

Mrs Stevens had been meaning to replace the tools in the potting shed for almost a week. She and the matrons had needed to cut the bottom of the trunk of the Christmas tree so that it would fit inside the stand they used every year, and she had shuffled around in that old shed for the best part of ten minutes trying to find a small saw. Eventually, she had found it and borrowed it – Ted worked limited hours during the winter season when the gardens were left quite fallow, so he wasn't about for her to make the request to borrow his tools. She ought to return it before he was back from his short break though. It was nearly eight o'clock in the evening, when she could return to her flat for the night and hand over to the night-shift matrons, so she decided to take the saw back to the potting shed before she forgot. She struggled with that damn noisy door at the dining room and made her way across the garden, letting herself into the potting shed, and finding the light switch just on the inside of the wall. She replaced the saw where she had found it and felt a cold shiver come over her. Colder than December wind – something chilled and prickly. It unnerved her and she turned in a hurry to leave the shed. She'd never liked the atmosphere in that dank space. As she got to the door, she sensed movement up in one of the second-floor windows. She squinted and as her eyes adjusted, she could see that it was four of the senior girls, Rosie and her group of friends. Mrs Stevens frowned for a moment and then raised her hand to wave at them. Their faces looked so worried and then suddenly erupted into laughter. Mrs Stevens thought how strangely they were acting, but perhaps they were excitable for the Christmas festivities coming up and probably – yes – they must have heard about the haunted stories concerning that changing room window on the second floor and they were up there getting inspiration for their spooky play. She laughed to herself and waved bigger, sillier, indulging them, laughing along as though she was in on the joke. Then she turned off the light and made her way back along the path to the dining room.

"Mrs Stevens!?" Emma gasped, "I can't believe how she is being with us."

"You really think it was her who left the note?" Lizzy asked, unconvinced.

"I think we don't give her enough credit for how funny she can be!" Dawn commented, "she well and truly had us!"

Rosie nudged Lizzy, "Remember she pranked us last night in the corridor with the humming and then jumping out of her office at us too?"

Lizzy nodded; she had to agree that Mrs Stevens seemed to be really getting into this 'spooky play' business.

Still giggling, Emma said, "Come on guys, let's go..."

Emma, Dawn and Rosie made their way out of the dark changing room. Lizzy stayed leaning against the stone wall and peering out into the landscaped gardens a moment longer. It was only a minute past eight – what if it hadn't been Mrs Stevens who left the note as a joke and the actual perpetrator was just waiting for the coast to be clear before making an appearance? Lizzy just wasn't utterly confident that Mrs Stevens would target Lizzy as the butt of her joke – she was closer aligned with Rosie and knew Emma to be the more jokey of the four of them. Why would she be aiming her joke at Lizzy, who was known to be a little more sensitive, studious and a bit of an over-thinker? It just didn't really add up. But as she watched the garden path silently, nobody else showed up. As she relaxed her focus, she became aware that she was sitting in this dark changing room all alone – her friends had left, and they had agreed not to switch on the lights so that they wouldn't be easily seen by whoever might appear in the garden. It could have been the realisation of this solitude, but Lizzy suddenly felt watched – a tingling on the back of her neck as though she was not alone in this room. She felt it so keenly that she wondered if perhaps one of the others hadn't left.

"Emma? Rosie? Dawn?" Lizzy called out, hoping it was just one of them. Nobody spoke up and as she glanced around behind her, she could see, in the light cast by the moon, the lockers which housed all the hockey equipment. They were large enough to fit a person who wanted to hide – Lizzy felt increasingly vulnerable and entertained thoughts of one of those locker doors creaking open and a hand appearing around the side. She knew her breathing had become laboured as she got herself into a panic. She shook her head – of course there was nobody in the lockers. Neither was there anybody in the room. She closed her eyes to regain control of her nerves. She breathed in slowly and exhaled even slower, just like her Grandma Eliza had taught her to do when she got worried about how far away her parents were, and her anxiety crept up to make her feel that something terrible would happen as they flew across the continents for business and may never make it home to her. Grandma Eliza knew how to help her relax. Lizzy breathed slowly three or four times and when she opened her eyes to the room, she felt instantly calmer – the changing room at night was just a room; the lockers were benign and nothing to fear. Satisfied, she bent down to retrieve the torch she had brought with her. Her hand shuffled about on the dusty floor, unable to find it. Perhaps one of her friends took it? No matter – she was going back down to the dorm now and would ask them. Lizzy decided to take one last look out at the potting shed before she left the changing room and as she turned to the window, there was a face outside, staring in at her. It was a man's face; he had a large head with a mop of unruly black hair, a tanned weathered complexion and wild, dark eyes. Lizzy screamed and fell backwards, sprawling on the floor, but even as she was looking at him, his face faded. Lizzy couldn't stop screaming; she scrambled to her feet and sprinted to the door, running out into the light of the hallway and practically threw herself down the corridor towards her dormitory. It was only as girls of all ages started emerging from their dorms in various pyjamas and nightdresses that Lizzy realised she had not stopped screaming. On hearing the commotion, Emma, Dawn and Rosie had also come out of their dorm and embraced Lizzy, all trying to shh and calm her. Then Vickie was there; their favourite matron – Vickie with her large, all-encompassing hugs, with offers of hot chocolate and marshmallows. They all helped Lizzy to her bed and got her under the covers even though she was still fully clothed. Lizzy wondered at this, through her shocked state, but understood when she saw that she was shaking violently, and her hands looked almost blue with cold.

"She must have been outside to have gotten herself this cold..." Vickie fussed as she pulled the duvet up to Lizzy's chin and put her palm to Lizzy's forehead to check for fever.

"Emma," Vickie instructed, "hold her hands like this and warm them" she demonstrated rubbing Lizzy's hands to get friction warming them. "Dawn – run to the kitchen staff and ask them to make a hot water bottle and a hot-chocolate; tell them where to bring it and then go to the nurse to ask her to attend with a thermometer."

Dawn dashed off to do so and Rosie stood at the foot of Lizzy's bed, feeling useless.

"What happened?" Rosie muttered.

"I saw a man – at the window..." Lizzy managed to stutter.

"Shh-shh" Vickie smoothed Lizzy's hair back from her sticky forehead.

"We were in the second-floor changing room," Rosie clarified in case it helped.

Vickie went still for a moment and peered over her shoulder at Rosie, "Really?"

Rosie nodded.

"Uh-huh," Vickie mused, as if this meant something to her.

Then she went back to shh-ing Lizzy and stroking her hair. Rosie really wanted to push Vickie for more information, but Lizzy was finally beginning to breathe more easily, and her eyes were starting to close. She needed quiet. Lizzy felt soothed by Vickie's presence, and she didn't remember anything more that evening as sleep enveloped her...

Although Lizzy felt entirely well in the morning, it was clear to her that her friends were tiptoeing around her. It was as if they were burning with questions for her but had been warned by the matrons not to ask. As they got ready for lessons, they made lame conversation about what they hoped to get for Christmas and where they would all be spending the festive break – topics they had discussed before in detail, so Lizzy knew they were just trying to fill in to cover the awkwardness. Eventually, Emma screwed up her face and asked, "Did you go down to the potting shed on your own after we all left the changing room, Lizzy?"

The other girls looked alarmed that Emma was

breaking the rule and asking, but then turned their attention to Lizzy – just as eager as Emma was, to hear her answer. Lizzy looked blankly at them all.

"Only," Emma continued, "Vickie said you were so cold, you must have gone outside – did you?"

Lizzy shook her head, "I didn't go outside."

Rosie stepped forward and put her hand on Lizzy's arm, in a gesture of support. "You told Vickie you saw a face at the window..."

Lizzy's chin dropped to her chest, as if she was holding in a sob, "I did," she whispered. When she looked up, all the girls were staring at her with their mouths open in shock.

"But then apparently when the nurse took my temperature, I had a fever – isn't that right?" Lizzy directed her question at Dawn, who nodded.

"So, it's possible I was hallucinating."

They all looked around at each other silently, unsure what to believe.

"I panicked – I couldn't find my torch because you guys took it when you left the changing room," Lizzy explained.

"Did we?" Rosie looked at the other two and they both shook their heads.

"We each had a torch, Lizzy. We all brought our own torch back to the dorm with us."

Lizzy frowned. "It definitely wasn't there – I couldn't find it."

"I'll go and fetch it for you at morning break," Emma offered.

"Not on your own, Emma – please" Lizzy begged. They all looked sadly at her – so much for her believing the whole thing was a delusion.

After breakfast, the girls walked along the postal corridor to the dining hall. Lizzy really didn't want to look at her pigeonhole, but it was unavoidable. She risked a sideways glance-and her torch was sat there. And with it, a note on thin, white paper. The others heard Lizzy gasp and followed her eyeline.

"Oh, your torch!" Emma exclaimed, "somebody found it and returned it – that's good."

Lizzy unwrapped the note and read aloud 'DID I SCARE YOU?' She looked up at her friends in dismay.

"There's no way this is from Mrs Stevens – she wouldn't do that after what happened to me last night!" Lizzy cried.

Rosie nodded, "Lizzy is right – the matrons would have told Mrs Stevens about Lizzy's fever and delirium, and she wouldn't continue the prank in this way..."

"But think about it," Dawn suggested, "isn't the likelihood that Mss Stevens added the note to the pigeon-hole at the end of her shift yesterday, to accompany her trick? She'd have planted it there as soon as she pulled the potting shed prank – which was *before* Lizzy had her little episode."

"Ah yes – that timeline tracks," Emma agreed.

"Oh," Rosie realised, "she probably feels awful about it now, knowing how terrible Lizzy felt later in the evening."

"The notes will stop now, though," Lizzy asserted, "it's been a bit weird – the house mistress getting herself so involved. After whatever-it-was that happened to me last night, I'm sure Mrs Stevens won't be initiating any more prank notes, so that's it now." Lizzy took a deep breath and let it shudder out, "I'm starving – let's go and have some warm porridge."

The girls continued down the corridor towards the dining hall and Lizzy tried not to wonder - if Mrs Stevens left the note early in the evening - how the torch got into her pigeon-hole late at night...

"Are you absolutely sure you're okay to do this today, Lizzy?" Rosie asked compassionately, as

Emma put the Ouija board onto the small table in the cloakroom.

Lizzy shrugged, "it seems whenever we try to kick off, there's an interruption. We just need to get the thing done."

"*Kicking off*" Rosie reprimanded, "is a football term. 'Blocking' is what we're doing with the play to get it started...but you're right. We *do* need to really sink our teeth into it – we don't have that long. The other teams are already discussing costumes..."

"So, we're all crowded around the board..." Dawn instigated the action.

"Well, actually, I realised that doesn't work for the big jumpy twist..." Rosie corrected.

The other girls looked at her questioningly.

"Ah, of course, we haven't gotten that far -" Rosie was toying with them. She fidgeted excitedly with a big grin on her face. "Okay, so what happens is, as the characters are playing on the board, they contact this matron called Rosemary and it's all spooky and atmospheric, really building up the tension for the audience, when suddenly an old lady - who is actually one of us, dressed up, obviously – shouts really loudly from the back of the hall "*Get to your rooms!!*" And all the audience jump so high and are so frightened."

"Cool! So, it's a jump-scare moment!" Emma enthused.

"I guess so," Rosie shrugged, "you like it?"

The girls all nodded.

"I vote Emma to be the old lady!" Lizzy volunteered.

"I thought *you* would want to be the old lady, Lizzy?" Emma queried, "so you can stand at the back of the hall and don't have to participate with the Ouija board?"

Lizzy shrugged, "You're the short arse out of all of us," she joked. She wouldn't tell Emma the real reason. She suspected it was Emma who was purposely moving the glass across the board to plant spooky messages and perhaps if Lizzy got herself on the board instead, all these unnerving pranks might stop.

The girls all laughed, pleased to see that Lizzy's mood had picked up.

Emma shrugged, "I can do old."

"Sorted then," Rosie smiled. "You two swap. Let's get on with the board part."

Lizzy shifted over into Emma's place by the board and took a deep breath as she placed her fingers onto the glass, mirroring Rosie and Dawn.

Immediately, the glass flew over to 'B'. Lizzy

looked up at Dawn to check her expression and then to Rosie – the two of them were exchanging a look. Lizzy had seen this before; and despite her feeling a little that their timing was inappropriate given the events of the previous evening, clearly this was a prank they were hell-bent on pursuing and she didn't want to cast herself as precious and over-sensitive, so she impulsively decided to play along. If you can't beat them, join them.

"Hmm," Lizzy inspected, looking between the two of them, "I seem to be the ghost's favourite, don't I?" she phrased it like a challenge and the three other girls grinned with anticipation.

Rosie clicked her tongue as the board messages again went off-script, but Dawn spelled out the letters as they were marked out "R.E.D.H.E.A.D.S.L.I.K.E.W.I.N.E".

"Redheads like wine?" Emma echoed from where she stood over by the door, awaiting her call to action, "that's a bit random."

The glass moved again, and Dawn continued to translate "D.O.Y.O.U.L.I.K.E.W.I.N.E.B?"

"What's Wineb?" Emma screwed up her face.

The others laughed "Wine, Emma!" Dawn called over, "The spirit is asking B if she likes wine...well, Lizzy? Are you going to answer?"

Lizzy shrugged, uncomfortably, "I don't really know – I had some champagne once at my dad's birthday party, but I've never really tried wine..." it seemed an odd question for her friends to pose – none of them had ever really been interested in alcohol. She'd heard of Senior girls before them in years before the pandemic who were always escaping campus to go and drink or bringing booze into their dorms and hoping they didn't get caught – none of her year-group seemed that interested. She'd recently read a science paper on the social studies of such a change and other similar shifts in adolescent behaviour that had been initiated through the enforced regulations of lockdown. She wondered momentarily if it was also now more likely for teenagers to pull insensitive pranks on their friends...

The glass started moving excitedly across the board and Dawn acted as its mouth-piece once again

"I.W.I.L.L.G.E.T.Y.O.U.W.I.N.E.

R.E.D.W.I.N.E.F.O.R.M.Y.R.E.D.H.E.A.D..."

"No, thank you guys – I don't want any wine, really."

Rosie looked up at Lizzy's protest, about to say something, but the glass began moving quickly again and this time Rosie read it aloud; "D.O.N.T.T.A.L.K.T.O.T.H.E.M.

T.A.L.K.T.O.M.E.

I.L.O.V.E.I.T.W.H.E.N.Y.O.U.T.A.L.K.T.O.M.E."

"Don't talk to them, talk to me – I love it when you talk to me? *Do* you talk to your ghost, Lizzy?" Emma joked.

Lizzy fished about for a jokey response, though the whole situation was starting to feel a lot less jokey. When – once more – the glass took on a life of its own.

"I.L.O.V.E.O.U.R.

P.R.I.V.A.T.E.M.O.M.E.N.T.S," Rosie spelled out.

"Oooh la la!" Emma teased, "*Private moments,* Lizzy? Who is this hunky ghost man of yours? He's got a real crush!"

Lizzy was about to remove her hand when the glass moved again. Rosie read aloud:

"O.U.R.M.O.M.E.N.T.I.N.

T.H.E.C.H.A.N.G.I.N.G.R.O.O.M.

W.I.N.D.O.W.Y.O.U.S.A.W.M.E"

Lizzy pulled her hand away in shock "Okay, that's enough!"

The other girls looked at her shocked.

"Please don't joke about the changing room – that isn't fair" Lizzy pleaded with them all, "I wasn't well..."

"Wait, it's still moving!" Rosie announced, and Lizzy watched as it spelled out the next sentence, with Rosie providing audio:

"A.N.D.W.H.E.N.Y.O.U.

R.E.A.D.J.A.N.E.S.D.I.A.R.Y"

Lizzy stood up with a loud intake of breath. Everybody removed their hands from the glass and stared up at her. Lizzy's hands were covering her mouth, and her face had dropped down the colour scale to a greyish pale. She was staring at the board in disbelief – then her eyes flicked to Rosie's.

Rosie's face went from entertained, to perplexed, to shocked then questioning and hurt.

"Lizzy? Did you read my diary?"

"Of course I didn't!" Lizzy's defensive response was too quick and too desperate.

"But..." Emma interjected, "to ask Lizzy if she actually read your diary, Rosie, is to suggest that we believe there is actually a spirit who has been watching Lizzy and who is actually talking to her through the board...?"

Dawn held her hands palm-out in surrender, "I swear I haven't been moving the glass..."

Rosie looked at her very suddenly. "Have you not?"

"What!?" the question came from Emma and Dawn.

"Wait!" Emma demanded, "so Rosie, you thought *Dawn* was pushing the glass?"

"Yes," said Rosie, "I didn't approve, but protesting seemed futile..."

"And you, Rosie, *weren't* pushing the glass either?" Emma clarified.

"I really wasn't..." Rosie held up her hands, looking nearly as pale as Lizzy.

They all looked to Lizzy, apologetic and worried. Lizzy was staring at the board as if in a trance and shaking her head very slightly.

"Did the spirit call you out, Lizzy?" Rosie pressed, "*did* you read my diary?"

"I didn't read your bloody diary, okay!?" Lizzy yelled and ran from the room.

They all sat silently for a moment and then Dawn busied herself in tidying away the Ouija board.

"If she didn't read my diary, then why was that the comment that made her react so strangely?" Rosie asked, almost haughtily.

"Lizzy isn't a snoop, Rosie," Emma protected her friend, "she's not herself right now, she's been unwell. Honestly, I think this has all just pushed her too far."

Dawn flapped about for a moment and then asked, "Did Lizzy take the glass?"

The three girls looked about the place as Emma explained "she can't have – she pushed open the door with both hands..."

They continued to look about, under the cloakroom benches, when there was a sudden loud crash of glass by the door. With a shocked scream from Rosie, they all turned to look across the room, at where the piercing smash had come from and - by the door where Lizzy had exited minutes before, there was a condensed pile of shattered glass.

As Lizzy escaped the cloakroom, she couldn't believe the board had told that she read Rosie's diary – was it possible that one of her friends saw her do it and this whole prank was payback for her dishonesty? If she believed that, she would hold her hands up and accept that she probably deserved this treatment, but there was absolutely no way anybody saw her – Rosie had been showering, Emma and Dawn had been with Mrs Stevens – nobody would have had their phone set up recording, because there was no need for surveillance of each other. But, Lizzy recalled, she *had* felt watched from the window and a shadow had strangely passed across – she remembered it with a shudder and as she did so, the image of the man's face from last night peering in through the changing room window at her slid sharply into her focus, making her want to cry out in alarm, so visceral was the flashback. Lizzy stopped and squeezed her eyes closed for a second and took a deep breath – her calming strategy didn't seem to be working this time. Then as she opened her eyes, she realised she was standing beside the postal pigeonholes, and her eyes instinctively went to check her cubby-hole. Oh, dear God. There, in the cavity, laid a bottle of red wine. As Lizzy forced herself to get her breathing under control, she heard a crash of glass from the cloakroom she had just vacated followed by a solo scream.

CHAPTER 8
1875

"Look at your tatty hair!" Clara scolded Betty, "take yourself back to your dormitory and brush it. What a disgrace you are..."

Betty's pale complexion blushed bright red, and tears filled her clear blue eyes, "Should I eat my porridge first, Ms Brown?"

"You may not – you're not fit to dine with your fellow students, looking like a raggy street urchin. You'll eat at lunch."

Clara watched as the girl swallowed hard – a knot of tension in her graceful, swan-like neck. She thought fleetingly how she'd like to take that beautiful neck in one fist and twist it to a furious red to match the girl's blushing face. She thought how easily such an elegant neck could break – and then realised that she was still standing over the girl, seething and that Betty was probably waiting for her to move before she could stand and depart as requested. So, Clara moved quickly to one side, making herself scarce down the row of girls who had all paused in the consumption of their porridge to stare at the drama unravelling before them.

"If you'd all prefer to go and brush your hair again like messy little Betty, then you'd better keep on staring," warned Clara frostily, and all faces were suddenly back at their bowls, spooning breakfast into their mouths. Clara felt a rush of power and marched back towards the kitchens.

"Was that really necessary, Ms Brown?" Rosemary whispered sharply as Clara passed her. Clara stopped and looked Rosemary dead in the eye – too close to her face to focus.

"You don't question me, Miss Faulkner."

"It's just that Betty's hair was neat and as brushed as any girl's here…why do you pick on her so?"

"What are you accusing me of, Miss Faulkner?" Clara spat as she spoke.

Rosemary dropped her eyes, realising she was powerless here, "Nothing, Ms Brown."

"I'm entirely pleased to hear it, Miss Faulkner. Now could you please clean up the spillage?" Clara whispered.

"What spillage?" Rosemary asked, but as she did so, she watched Clara's hand stick out and deliberately push a bowl of porridge off the countertop and empty its contents all over the wooden floor.

The days at Holly House weren't joyful anymore. Rosemary used to wake in the mornings excited to see who she would get to talk to, what she might learn, how she might be able to help the students. Now she woke dreading the immoral behaviour she might witness, the criticism she may have to endure and the unfairness she may be forced to turn a blind eye to.

The darkness made it even harder – Rosemary usually loved Christmas time; it was her favourite season and in other years the dark mornings were brightened by the holly-berries decorating the wreaths on the bannisters, the tangible excitement of the girls anticipating going home to their families, to indulgent food and to presents. Being up for three hours before it even got light outside was no challenge to her when her soul was fed by such happiness in the boarding house. But now. Rosemary knew it was five AM and that it was cold, but she had extra woollen layers sent from her grandmother that she could put on – that it was dark, but she would carry her lantern as she went about her morning duties until light came – that she felt sad and victimised….and there was no salve for that. She couldn't lift her spirits enough to get out of bed. This was so unlike Rosemary, and as she lay there thinking how impossible the prospect of getting up felt, it alarmed her just *how* unlike herself she felt and that made her stay in bed a while longer. By the time she felt able to move at all, it was twenty-past-five, and she groaned as she realised how much harder everything would be as a result of her tardiness. She had so many chores to complete before waking the girls at six AM – there wasn't time to do it all, which meant she wouldn't be able to take a break today. She held her head in her hands and felt like crying, but no tears would come.

As she pushed herself to stride down the corridor towards the dining room, she made herself hum as she usually would. She thought it might help her to feel better, although it was so forced and probably sounded more like a funeral march than anything light and melodic. It also had the unfortunate effect of alerting Ms Clara Brown to her presence. As she passed, Clara's office door sprang open.

"Late this morning, aren't we, Rosemary?"

Rosemary couldn't repress the sigh that escaped her lips, "I'll work through my break to make up the time, Ms Brown."

"Darn right you will –oh and ask the pantry staff to fix me some tea as you pass," Clara instructed before disappearing back inside her office. There was no way Rosemary was going to request the hard-working pantry staff, in their most pressured hour of the day, to break off from their scheduled work to make Ms Brown tea. Which meant that Rosemary herself would have to do it; another item to add to her already-overflowing 'to do' list.

As she passed the small corridor window overlooking the lawn and saw that the sky was still pitch-black and the stars still bright, she found herself wishing it was the other end of the day – that it was evening, and she was on her way to bed. She hadn't slept at all well recently; fear that George Stone could be stalking the halls, and she had no way of protecting the girls from him. Nights only brought fear; but she would take that fear now happily, if it only meant she could sleep – oh, let it be night. Then she felt guilty; Rosemary had been raised to appreciate the beauty in every moment and never take it for granted – but she had a bad feeling about today.

Rosemary kept her head down for most of the day – she tried not to engage with any of the staff, which was uncharacteristic of her. She would help the children as and when they needed, but she did the bare minimum, feeling incapable of any extra shine or energy.

Ms Brown called an inspection – this happened on occasion and Rosemary rolled her eyes that it would *have* to be today...she did a quick runaround of all the dormitories, checking the girls had their hair tied appropriately; that their fingernails were clean; their smocks neat and their shoes polished. She paid particular attention to Betty, knowing that Clara would take any opportunity to pull the girl to pieces regarding her appearance. So as the girls lined up, standing tall and proud in the recreation hall for Ms Brown to walk down each line, checking the appearance of them all, Rosemary breathed a sigh of relief as Clara passed Betty without comment. She allowed her back to relax against the wall behind her, grateful for a moment that no cruelty had been dealt out.

"Before you all go," Clara boomed upon completion of the row-by-row inspection. Rosemary was immediately back on high alert, shifting her back away from the wall.

"*Somebody* here," Clara continued, "thinks themselves a little fancy."

As Clara paused for dramatic effect, she took slow, clipped footsteps up and down the rows of girls. Rosemary looked to Betty, concerned and noted that Betty's eyes flicked up to Rosemary, with a pleading expression for help. Rosemary felt adrenaline coursing through her as Clara took her time coming to her next statement.

"*Somebody* here, thinks themselves not merely a girl, but a *lady*..."

Rosemary saw the flush of red beginning to work itself over Betty's porcelain skin as panic rose in her. Rosemary had no idea where Clara's accusatory tone was headed, but she knew it was coming in Betty's direction any minute now –

"Betty Grainger!" Clara screeched, turning about as though she were in the military and pointing at Betty, whose mouth fell open. "Step this way," Clara instructed.

A few of the girls mumbled in consternation as Betty awkwardly made her way to the front of the hall where Clara now stood.

When Betty arrived in front of her, eyes wide and innocent, Clara made a big display of looking the girl up and down.

"How old are you, Betty?" Clara barked.

"Fifteen, Ms Brown," Betty replied quietly.

"And what is different about you, compared to the other fifteen-year-old girls in the room?" Clara enquired, gesturing to the hall full of girls, suggesting she take a look around.

Rosemary saw the glint of panic in Betty's eyes as her vision roamed the room, desperate to find the right answer, but clearly at a total loss.

"I...maybe..." Betty fidgeted, trying to find a disparity, "perhaps I am a little taller?"

"No," Clara slapped this suggestion down. "You are tall, but so too are Jessica Moriarty and Alexandra Salcombe. Try again."

Betty's eyes were now filling with tears as she stared around the room at all the faces, willing her on – Betty was well-liked and the discomfort of everybody watching her was palpable. Rosemary wanted nothing more than to run to Betty, embrace her protectively and yell at Clara to stop this humiliation – she almost did, but remembered how both Clara and George would happily vouch for her being of unstable mind and potentially losing not only her role, but her freedom, if they reported her as insane. Regular people were wrongfully sent to sanitoriums all the time; whilst this was painful to watch, she could not sacrifice her freedom for it.

"I'm sorry, Ms Brown" Betty finally sniffed, "I really don't know what makes me different from the other fifteen-year-olds..."

"These!" Clara yelled, shockingly pointing at Betty's chest. "You are a child, pretending you are a woman! Go now to the bathroom and remove whatever it is you have filled your vest with!"

Betty stared open-mouthed in horror at the house mistress.

"What is it? Tissue paper? Stockings? What have you stuffed upon your chest to make it look as though you are a woman?"

Betty began to sob now; visibly and audibly. "Please, Ms Brown – I haven't...it's not..."

Clara frowned at the girl, entirely without compassion.

Rosemary could not believe what she was witnessing – not only was this the most degrading display of condescension she had ever seen, but it was also completely without foundation; many of the girls – even some aged thirteen – had begun to grow breasts. Some were even much larger than Betty. This argument was not only grotesque, but entirely without grounds.

"Ah," Clara concluded, playing that she had *only just realised* what Betty was trying to explain, "then I think you had better get yourself to the school nurse, Betty, because your body is clearly growing all wrong."

Betty didn't wait – she turned for the door and ran. Rosemary followed straight after her, lifting her skirts so as not to trip down the corridor and as she rounded the newel post, she almost fell over Betty, who was curled in a ball on the bottom step, her delicate shoulders wracking with sobs. Rosemary bundled her into an embrace under her arm so she could help her to take the steps.

"Come with me – before she lets everybody out of the hall. Come -"

Betty brought herself to standing and the two of them bustled up the stairs to Rosemary's flat, and Betty once again collapsed into the cosy armchair.

"I am so, so, very sorry, Betty," Rosemary shook her head as she stroked the girl's red hair from her furrowing brow.

"But it wasn't your fault," Betty protested.

"I should have stepped in – I should have stopped her," Rosemary muttered, partially to herself, "and I'm sorry on behalf of the school staff – there is no way Ms Brown should have spoken to you in the way that she did."

Rosemary handed Betty her handkerchief and knelt on the floor beside the armchair.

"Betty – I need to know that you understand..." she waited for Betty to look her in the eye, "that what she said is absolute nonsense. That your body is growing just as it should. That there is nothing to be ashamed of."

Betty just stared at her with her wide, wet, blue eyes.

"Can you let me know that you understand that, Betty?"

It took a moment, but then Betty nodded, uncertainly.

"But then why did she say that?" Betty's voice trembled as she asked, "if there isn't anything wrong with me, why did she say that?"

"You are a beautiful girl, Betty. Ms Brown hates beautiful girls, because she sees them as competition," Rosemary decided to herself she had nothing to lose by being honest with this girl, who deserved authenticity, especially after what she had just endured.

"Competition? What do you mean?" Betty questioned.

Rosemary's heartbeat harder at the girl's words, which further reinforced her naivety and innocence in this whole predicament. Rosemary took a deep breath.

"Has George Stone the gardener bothered you at all since we last spoke?"

Betty blinked hard once, then a loud, wet cry escaped her, and she buried her face in the handkerchief once again. "He leaves me notes, all the time. With my post. In my pigeon-hole. Asking me to come and visit him...but I don't want to, Miss Faulkner; I'm scared of him. He's an adult so I know I should do as he says, but I'm too frightened. And he says he'll hurt me if I don't agree to be his friend and I'm just so scared..." all these words tumbled out of Betty in gasping breaths punctuated by sobs.

"Wait!" Rosemary stopped Betty mid-flow, "He may be an adult, but you most certainly do *not* need to do as he says. He is not a teacher. He is a bad man."

Betty stilled, "Is he?" her voice had taken on a

whisper that had some power in it – some self-belief that her doubts about him had been valid.

Rosemary nodded once, sadly. "I'm sorry to say I believe he is, yes."

"Then they are both bad," Betty concluded, "Ms Brown is bullying me, Miss Faulkner. She's been bullying me for weeks. I haven't known what to do about it but now everybody saw what she did today – will you help me?"

Rosemary paused – she would need to be careful about committing to anything that could incriminate her. "How can I help you, Betty?"

"Please report Ms Brown to the Headmistress for me?"

Rosemary's shoulders sank. "You do know that the Headmistress and the Housemistress are related, Betty? They are sister-in-law to each other and close confidantes..."

"But surely she can't ignore an accusation of bullying?" Betty protested, righteously.

Rosemary looked down at the ground and then apologetically shrugged, "I'm afraid I really don't know..."

Betty's bravado of moments before sagged.

"In any case," Rosemary added, "an accusation would be stronger coming from you – the pupil.

Your parents pay the school fees. If I complain, they are likely to simply remove me from my position and nothing would get done to help you."

"Oh, I couldn't have that!" Betty reached out to grab Rosemary's hand in solidarity.

The two of them were still and quiet a moment.

"Unless..." Rosemary began, and Betty looked up at her hopefully, "there is an accusation the Headmistress would be highly unlikely to ignore..."

Betty stared at Rosemary, eager for her to continue.

"If you felt you could write down what happened to you with regard to George Stone the gardener..." Rosemary said it softly, knowing this was a triggering memory for Betty. Betty pulled her hand away as if she'd been stung.

"He cannot be allowed to continue with this behaviour, Betty. If I report him, they could just retire me from the school, as I said – it would be easier to dismiss a female matron as the problem, than to have to deal with a report of inappropriate behaviour from a male member of staff... If *you* report him, as the victim and as the daughter of a client, they will have to listen – they will have to take your allegation seriously."

Betty nodded, solemnly.

"But that won't stop Ms Brown from bullying me?" Betty frowned.

"Ah but I believe it will – when she sees that you are not afraid to speak up and call out people who are in the wrong, she will fear for her job. She will begin to behave herself around you – I'm quite sure of it."

"So, if I agree," Betty tentatively queried, "to write down what George Stone did -"

"And what he is still doing – if you have kept any of the notes he has sent to you? Include them with your letter, as evidence..."

"I have. I can," Betty was warming to the idea of being able to prove George's crimes against her, "I really don't feel brave enough to take the letter to the Headmistress..."

"That's where I *can* help," Rosemary offered a smile, "it is my job to personally deliver the Headmistress her post each day, so I shall personally ensure it's safe arrival – and will in fact flag it as a priority item for her to read."

Betty took a deep breath and nodded decisively.

"Do we have a plan?" Rosemary asked hopefully.

"We do," Betty agreed, "I will write the letter as soon as I can and give it to you sometime tomorrow."

"It's likely to be delivered to the Headmistress the following day then," Rosemary planned, thinking out loud, "be prepared that you may be called out of class to talk with the Headmistress once she has read it, but you can request that you'd like me to attend any meetings with you, if that would help you to feel more supported?"

"Oh yes please!" Betty smiled through her teary eyes.

They both jumped as the loud bell tolled for dinner.

"Wipe your eyes, go and splash your face with water, then go down to eat – can you do that for me, Betty?" Rosemary asked, bowing to meet the young girl's eyes.

"I'd rather stay here," Betty cowered.

"You need to eat. You need food for strength, and you need to show her that she has not shaken you," Rosemary assured her.

"But she has..." Betty's tears threatened again.

"Don't let her see it. Walk into that dining room with your head held high. All your friends will be there supporting you. And I'm at dinner service tonight, so I'll be keeping an eye out for you." Rosemary encouraged.

Betty went to stand "I'll try..."

"Good girl. You're very brave. Braver than the likes of Ms Brown could ever hope to be," she threw Betty a wink as she showed her to the door. Rosemary watched the poor girl go, then hurried to splash her own face with water, spritzed herself with her refreshing homemade rose perfume and ran down the stairs to conduct the dinner service.

At last, she had potential to overcome this situation – Betty's accusation would surely mean George Stone would be dismissed and perhaps in the chaos of it all, his relationship with Clara Brown would come to light, causing her dismissal also. For the first time in weeks, Rosemary felt her heart lift a little and as she navigated the corridor past the office of her nemesis, she allowed herself to hum a little.

CHAPTER 9
PRESENT DAY

Lizzy burst into Vickie's office, almost forgetting to knock as she fell into the room. If it had been Mrs Steven's office she would most certainly have been reprimanded, but Vickie simply spun around on her wheelie chair in surprise and then, upon seeing Lizzy's fretful expression, exclaimed in her soft Irish accent, "Goodness child – whatever is the matter?" Her eyes came to rest upon the bottle of red wine in Lizzy's hand, "an early Christmas gift for me?" she was jesting – Vickie always was – but she stood to hug Lizzy as she could see she was in a terrible state.

"Come and sit down…" Vickie offered Lizzy the cosy armchair in the corner and Vickie went to switch on her little kettle on the sideboard and shuffled about with a sachet of hot chocolate powder, selected a cup with a Christmas elf on it and then piled herself back onto her wheelie chair and wheeled it forwards so she was next to Lizzy, with a childish little 'whoop!' as she arrived there.

"I feel like I'm going crazy…" Lizzy sobbed into her hands.

Vickie flourished a tissue from a box on the side as the kettle reached boiling point and noisily trundled on its base.

"You had a fever last night," Vickie justified and from seemingly nowhere produced a thermometer. She held it by Lizzy's forehead and upon a green reading of 37.4 degrees, shrugged. "So tell me."

"I don't think I can…" Lizzy apologised, "not without getting my friends into trouble."

"Are you in danger?" Vickie checked.

"I don't know…possibly? But not really, no," Lizzy replied, realising that her answers were totally unclarified but uncertain how else to proceed.

"The secrets you need to keep in order to refrain from outing your friends – will they hurt anybody?" Vickie rephrased.

Lizzy thought on this for a moment, then confidently said "no."

"Then tell me the parts that won't get anybody into trouble," Vickie suggested fairly.

"Our Christmas play" Lizzy began, "it's a ghost story."

"Ah yes! So I've heard from Mrs Stevens – very spooky and mysterious!" Vickie bounced about on her seat.

"Well, that's the thing," Lizzy tried to explain, "the spookiness and mystery doesn't want to stay on script."

Vickie stopped her excitable bouncing and came to a still. "What do you mean?"

"I'm going to sound mad…" Lizzy carefully put the bottle of red wine on the floor.

"Try me," proffered Vickie.

"I hear humming in the corridor off the dining room," Lizzy began, and Vickie simply nodded.

"There's a really strong smell of roses all along that corridor too – but particularly around the post room and Mrs Steven's office."

Again, Vickie nodded, then she took a deep breath and said, quite matter-of-factly "Well, sure, that'll be Rosemary Faulkner."

"What!?" Lizzy accidentally kicked the bottle of wine as she jumped – it fell to the floor and rolled noisily along the wooden floorboards before coming to rest on the other side of the small room. They both watched it and then Lizzy turned her attention back to Vickie.

"The Matron who worked here back in 1875," Vickie clarified.

"I've heard about her!" Lizzy exclaimed, "we did some research for our play…"

"Sure, that'll be her. She's harmless" Vickie mused, smiling, "I've seen her a few times – happy soul, going about her work."

"You've *seen* her!?" Lizzy couldn't believe what she was hearing. Vickie simply smiled and nodded, then stood to finish making Lizzy's hot chocolate.

As her back was turned, stirring in the milk, her voice took on a more serious tone, "I don't believe they're *all* harmless though, Lizzy."

"All?" Lizzy asked, exasperated, "you mean there are *more?*"

"Oh, come now – I think you've seen one yourself," she paused, "haven't you?" Vickie handed Lizzy the cup of hot chocolate, dotted with mini marshmallows floating on top "The man at the changing room window?"

Lizzy could only stare at Vickie, open-mouthed.

"That'll be George Stone. Not so friendly, that

one. A predator by all accounts," she nodded to reinforce her point, "stay clear of him, Lizzy."

"I'm trying to but – the play – it's like we've invited him in somehow…" Lizzy panicked.

"How so?" Vickie frowned.

"That's what I can't tell you…" Lizzy bit her lip.

"Well, change the play." Vickie concluded quite firmly.

"We can't…Rosie wrote it. You know how precious she is about her performances," Lizzy tried to explain.

"Oh dear. Then it will be tricky. But I'd strongly advise you change it, Lizzy," Vickie warned.

"I don't think it would change anything now anyway – it started with the play but now it's gotten so much bigger…"

"Can you just tell me the whole situation?" Vickie leaned forward, pleading.

"I just can't, Vickie. I think I need to try and work this out on my own. But at least now I know I'm not going mad and to hear you validate that they exist – that you've seen them too. I don't know; it helps somehow? Thank you…" Lizzy took one sip of the hot chocolate and then set it on a side-table, before standing to go to the door.

"What's with the wine bottle?" Vickie asked before she left.

"It appeared in my pigeon-hole. You can have it – Happy Christmas…" Lizzy shrugged sadly.

Vickie came to stand up as quickly as her rounded body allowed her to "I'm here, Lizzy – if you need any help with this. Please know that you can come to me. It's why I'm here."

Lizzy smiled and turned to go but Vickie suddenly cried out, pointing at the floor, "Where did the wine bottle go?"

Lizzy looked to where Vickie was pointing, only to see that it had, indeed, disappeared. She felt as if these occurrences didn't even faze her anymore.

"I guess George Stone wanted it back…"

CHAPTER 10
1875

There was a knock on the door of the flat as Rosemary refreshed for dinner service the next day – this was not a common occurrence; the children were not allowed to disturb the matrons when they were in their living quarters unless there was an emergency, so Rosemary dashed to answer it.

"I'm sorry," Betty said sheepishly, handing over a white envelope addressed very neatly to *Mrs Brown, Headmistress of Meadowbank School – IMPORTANT*. "I know I'm not supposed to disturb you up here, but I've been clutching the letter all day trying to find a discreet opportunity to deliver it to you…"

"Oh, it's no matter at all," hushed Rosemary and put out her hand to receive the letter.

"I left it unsealed – I hoped that you might kindly read it this evening and then only deliver it to the Headmistress tomorrow if you think it is all as it should be..." Betty implored.

"I will do so, if you are happy for me to read the contents," Rosemary nodded.

"Of course," Betty fidgeted and then flew to give Rosemary a hug, "thank you for your support, Miss Faulkner. I really didn't know what I was going to do – I thought I might need to leave the school, and I really didn't want to have to do that..."

Rosemary hugged her right back "I only wish you'd confided in me earlier," she pulled away and gestured with the letter, "now I shall read this tonight, deliver it tomorrow and – I just want you to be aware that this probably won't be a nice, neat finish; it could get emotional and messy, but remember that you are doing the right thing."

"Thank you, Miss Faulkner," Betty smiled – a beam Rosemary had missed recently – and she tiptoed off down the corridor.

Rosemary looked down again at the neat handwriting and peeked inside the envelope, to see not only the formal handwriting paper, but a few snippets of thin, cheap paper, which she assumed to be George's notes. She clicked her tongue at how many there appeared to be and returned to her flat, closing the door behind her. If only she had looked up, she might have seen Clara on the floor above, outside her own apartment, staring down from the balcony, having caught the tail-end of Rosemary and Betty's conversation and drawing her own conclusions...

Rosemary became aware of a kerfuffle in the corridor outside Clara's office as she re-set the dining room chairs after dinner, ready for the following day's breakfast sitting. She caught a glimpse of Marianne Atkinson looking fraught and prayed to herself that it wasn't another of George Stone's antics upsetting one of the girls, but then she heard the words *'missing from my room'* and breathed a sigh of relief. As the crowd disappeared from the corridor, she put it to the back of her mind – she was anxious to get back to her own room that evening and read the letter from Betty outlining George Stone's inappropriate behaviours for her to deliver to the Headmistress the next day, and she thought of not much else as she realigned the tables and stacked the wooden chairs neatly together. This exercise warmed her up in the winter months and she was grateful for it – in the summer it was a heavy chore which would leave her sweating and uncomfortable. Today it was a welcome task, a mindless activity for her to focus her mind on what she must do the following day; she would probably accompany Betty's letter with a word to the Headmistress that a serious allegation had been made to her by the child, concerning the content of the letter – that would ensure it would be read.

Suddenly the commotion was back and this time, Clara, Marianne Atkinson, two reluctant-looking matrons who were friends of Rosemary's and a warden, all trampled into the hall.

"Rosemary Faulkner," Clara shouted across the space and Rosemary was immediately alarmed – Clara used her full name in front of a student, and she had brought with her a cavalry. What was going on? Rosemary gently replaced the chair she had just lifted, back down to the floor.

"I am here to inform you that we will be carrying out a full search of your living quarters, as we have reason to believe you have stolen Marianne Atkinson's silver locket which has gone missing from her dormitory."

"Wh-what!?" the announcement was so unexpected, so mis-aligned with anything that made sense. Rosemary had never stolen anything in her life – whyever would they jump to a presumption that she had taken the locket?

"Why would you think *I* had taken it?" Rosemary stammered.

"You visited all of the dormitories yesterday ahead of the student inspection, did you not?" Clara boomed.

"I did..." Rosemary was shaking her head, none of this making any sense.

"And you disappeared for a considerable amount of time between the inspection itself and dinner service yesterday afternoon – this was noted by several staff who missed your presence. You were unaccounted for during this extended period of time, and I put it to you that you had seen Marianne's silver locket during the inspection preparation, then returned to steal it and covet it in your own flat." Clara stated accusingly.

"No – I never would do that!" Rosemary protested, her face growing red with shame and anger.

"Whether or not you would do that shall be proved within the hour, once we have conducted a full search of your living quarters," Clara concluded and she turned to proceed down the corridor, with her assembled staff following behind her hesitantly, a couple of them shooting apologetic glances at Rosemary as they did so.

Rosemary wanted to say something with bravado, such as *'that's fine, you won't find anything'* but she had a distinctive sinking feeling that this whole debacle was being staged by Clara and that she would not be going to such trouble to create drama unless she had a specific plan. Rosemary abandoned her dining room duties and rushed after them.

As the group reached Rosemary's flat and Clara used her master key to enter, Clara announced "I'll check the bedroom!"

Clara rushed ahead to the bedroom and headed straight to the bed; she quickly took the silver locket from her pocket and slipped it under the pillow, before making her way hastily to the desk by the window. There was the letter she had seen Betty handing over to Rosemary earlier that day. She looked towards the door to check none of the others were coming through yet; she could hear them busying themselves in the snug area, where there were furnishings and bookshelves to be checked and another of them in the bathroom – she had a moment. Clara quickly took the letter from its envelope and several other thinner papers fluttered down to the ground. She cursed under her breath as she scooped down to retrieve them and unfolded one as she stood – she recognised the handwriting instantly as George's and her breath caught as she read the words '*Meet me in the potting shed at 8pm*'. Clara had received notes just like this, in the same hand and she suddenly felt as though she had a golf ball in her throat, she couldn't swallow, but she had no time to process this revelation right now and took all the smaller notes, pushing them deep into her pocket, then opened the formal letter as she sneaked another quick look at the door. Her eyes picked out one sentence in her hurry '*….report Mr George Stone the Gardener for inappropriate behaviour towards me...*' and then, hearing the others approaching the bedroom in their continued search, one other sentence '*...tried to touch me between my legs...*' Clara gasped but had to close the letter in a rush, placing it hurriedly back into its envelope and shoved it into her pocket moments before the warden pushed through the bedroom door – to an unknowing eye, it simply looked as though she were moving things around on the desk in her hunt for the locket.

"Any luck in here, Ms Brown?" asked the uniformed warden.

"Not in the desk," Clara breathed, hoping he couldn't tell how flustered she was, "I haven't searched over there yet -" she gestured in the general direction of the bed, and he walked over to move the bed linen.

"Perhaps I was wrong...poor Rosemary, being wrongly accused, I will need to apologise," Clara held her hand to her chest in mock remorse, when the warden suddenly straightened up.

"I think I may have found it, Ms Brown," he stood with a silver chain and sparkling locket dangling from his hand.

The others heard his announcement and darted into the bedroom to see it with their own eyes – there were gasps of dismay and disbelief.

"Oh dear," Clara mourned, "what a bitter disappointment."

The staff ushered through Marianne Atkinson from the back of their crowd and Marianne stepped forward confirming, "Yes, that's my locket...but I'm quite sure that Miss Faulkner wouldn't have..."

"Miss Faulkner has clearly deceived us all with her seemingly pleasant demeanour," Clara blustered, ushering everybody out of the flat to where Rosemary stood on the landing outside her room. Nobody would meet her eye as they emerged from the room. Rosemary bit at the inside of her mouth until she could taste the metallic tang of blood. Clara stepped confidently from the room and met Rosemary's eye.

"We found Marianne's silver locket under your pillow, Miss Faulkner," Clara confirmed with a glint of enjoyment in her eye. "I will be reporting your illegal antics to the Headmistress, and you shall report to her tomorrow first thing. Refrain from carrying out any of your usual school duties until further notice. Please stay in your room. Food will be brought up to you later. Do not leave your room until such a time as we can reach a decision as to what action should be taken."

Rosemary felt hot tears upon her face and her hands were shaking.

"But I didn't …. I honestly didn't…" she protested weakly, knowing that the evidence to the contrary would mean she would have to endure this confinement.

"Will you – be calling the police?" Rosemary whimpered and hoped the question didn't cast her as genuinely guilty in the eyes of her friends gathered there.

"I will leave that up to the Headmistress to

decide when you stand before her tomorrow," Clara spoke haughtily.

"Am I under house-arrest?" Rosemary asked, pitifully.

"Not officially. But if you leave your room, I may have to consider calling the police *before* speaking with the Headmistress," Clara pouted, then turned on her heel and began to descend the stairs.

Rosemary didn't want to stand here with this group of people thinking she was a dirty thief, so she quickly headed into her flat. Julie caught her by the arm and squeezed it. "I don't believe you did this, Rosemary," she whispered, before Rosemary shot her a sad smile and disappeared into her room.

It didn't matter whether Julie believed her or not – if you were found guilty of theft, you would be sent to prison. Julie knew it and Rosemary knew it. It wasn't just a case of potentially losing her job anymore. She could be convicted for this. Rosemary would be holding court with the Headmistress tomorrow as planned, but not discussing the topic she had hoped to. Rosemary was now the suspected perpetrator, not George Stone. Oh! – Rosemary suddenly remembered the letter standing vulnerably on the desk, where it would surely have been seen during the search. She ran to her desk –

unsurprised to see that it was no longer there. She didn't need to think hard to guess who would have taken it. Rosemary sank to her floor, holding her face in her hands. Her life, as she knew it, was ruined.

In the privacy of her apartment, Clara emptied her pockets of the thin notes of paper and the thicker matte of the formal letter. Framing Rosemary had gone well – there was no doubt in Clara's mind that Alice would dismiss Rosemary with immediate effect when they met tomorrow morning. The problem of a meddling matron would no longer be the bane of Clara's existence. But now Clara had these notes written in George's hand, accompanied by a formal letter from a student accusing him of inappropriate behaviour and this presented a whole other issue for her to contend with, which made her face burn bright with embarrassment and fury. Could George *really* be writing notes to this Betty girl? Clara had decided Betty was infatuated with George – that she consistently approached him with her flirtatious femininity, and he was in the uncomfortable position of having to rebuff her advances whilst not wanting to appear rude. Clara opened up each of the cheap paper notes, flattening them against her desk, reading each one as she opened them:

I think you are so pretty.
Do you like wine? I have some for you.
Meet me in the potting shed at 8pm.
I can't stop thinking about you.
I love spending time with you, beautiful lady.

Wait! A judder of joy suddenly fluttered through Clara's chest – these notes were all *exactly the same* as notes she herself had received from George. She was sure of it. She hadn't kept them, in case it alerted the staff to the fact they were having a relationship – she had thrown them in various rubbish bins about the boarding house; if found they could have been *from* anybody *to* anybody. What if Betty, or Rosemary had been collecting the notes, in order to complain about George? The irony of her lover being framed, by the very person she had just framed was not lost on Clara. She held her head in her hands, laughing at the bizarre turn of events.

Clara felt instantly guilty for having suspected George, even for a moment. She wanted to run to him, but that would have to wait until later – for now, she needed to uphold complete professionalism and focus entirely on getting Rosemary excluded from her position at Meadowbank School.

She was so close now and felt triumphant, not only in finally getting rid of Rosemary, but in vindicating George. He was a good, upstanding man and – despite their difference in social status – perhaps one day they might be officially together. Clara grinned to herself and decided not to even to read the lies Betty had included in her letter. It would only feel like another layer of betrayal of George and might risk laying seeds of doubt in her mind once again. She filed the letter away in her top desk drawer and went to complete the duties that Rosemary would not be permitted to do this evening.

"Ms Brown informs me that a student's silver locket was found under your pillow in your bedroom, Miss Faulkner – what do you have to say on the matter?"

Alice Brown, Headmistress. Rosemary's only past dealings with her had been ones of impressive interviews, welcoming commendations, social niceties – never this. Never on the disapproving side of this intimidating tyrant. Her whole voice was different; deeper, sterner. Rosemary felt quite sick. She hadn't been able to eat since yesterday lunchtime – the last time her world still seemed relatively normal. She had no appetite, but she also felt weak, shaky, nauseated. Her brain couldn't catch up with the situation – how had she, an upstanding, honest, helpful, compassionate and well-loved house matron suddenly been cast as a dishonest thief?

"I did not steal the locket, Mrs Brown," Rosemary conjured up the energy to respond.

"Then what do you propose happened to get the locket from Marianne Atkinson's dormitory - to your mattress?" Mrs Brown was unflinching.

Rosemary risked a glance across at Clara, who had marched Rosemary over to the Headmistresses' office like a criminal. Clara looked back at her through satisfied, narrowed eyes. If the two women weren't related, Rosemary would most definitely be calling it out that she had been framed by Clara Brown. But there was no way Mrs Brown would believe her, so she just looked down at the ground – as a tear dropped to the floor and she simply mumbled, "I don't know..."

"Very well. If there is no alternative explanation, then it seems clear you stole the locket from the student..." Mrs Brown concluded.

"I really didn't!" Rosemary protested through her sobs.

Mrs Brown spread her palms, demonstrating

that she was at a loss as to how to proceed without further information.

"I need to give this some thought," Mrs Brown stated, "Rosemary Faulkner, you have been a reliable and loyal member of staff for many years, and it is certain your loss will be felt keenly by students and staff alike, but I'm afraid I have no choice other than to request that you retire from your position. We cannot have theft amongst our community. It will not be tolerated. You have three days to vacate your flat. On the matter of whether or not the police will be involved – this is where I need to consider the situation further. I will ruminate on this and call you back in for a meeting once I have decided the best way to proceed." Mrs Brown nodded curtly and that was it.

Rosemary's career ended. Her home being taken from her. Her community of friends inaccessible. Her reputation destroyed. Her freedom hanging in the balance. Her sanity possibly called into question.

That one sentence from this woman and Rosemary had been ruined.

She fell to the floor. She hated drama – it wasn't intentional, she was just unable to stay upright. She was aware of tongues clicking and declarations of inconvenience as she was removed from the room. It was only half-way across the lawn that she gained awareness enough to look at who the two people were, who were escorting her by lifting an arm each and partially taking her weight as she tried to stumble along. On one side was the warden who had witnessed her humiliation yesterday and on the other – she physically recoiled as she saw him there – was George Stone. He grinned crookedly at her as she gasped and then she felt him graze his free hand across the side of her chest. She retched on to the grass – her empty stomach not bringing up any content. She wasn't sure if she passed out then, but she didn't remember any more after that until waking later in the evening on her bed that would soon not be her bed, in her flat that was no longer her home.

Rosemary had no idea what the time was – only that it was dark, and it was quiet. She hadn't really given much thought to what she was about to do. There seemed no point in considering it for long – even if Mrs Brown decided not to call the police, Rosemary would be unable to get another job without any references from the past decade. She would end up in the workhouse. That was not an existence she could tolerate. As she left her flat and made her way up the stairs, she thought about how, since her parents had died, she had always tried so hard to be bright and sunny for everyone around her; lifting spirits, making beautiful scents to share, supporting young children who needed affection and guidance, humming and singing to make her day better even when she didn't feel like singing. And it was all for nothing. Why had she worked so hard to lift everybody around her if this was how it all ended?

She was at the top floor. She opened the window to its widest point and stepped up on to the desk. As she looked down, she thought how ironic it was that directly below – four floors down – was the lawned entrance to the dining room; the spot where all the trouble had started. She didn't want to think any more.

She just let herself fall. A drastic sudden rush of cold wind to her face and then it all went black.

CHAPTER 11
PRESENT DAY

Lizzy hadn't been sleeping well. The man's face haunted her dreams and often she would wake from light slumber feeling freezing cold, fizzing with frost, despite the radiator being turned up to the maximum. The others were sweltering, but she just couldn't get warm.

She felt constantly watched during the day – Emma had even asked her in English class why she kept looking over her shoulder. She hadn't even been aware of doing it.

Lizzy couldn't walk the postal corridor now without the strong scent of rose assaulting her senses and she heard the humming there always – even on occasions the others said they couldn't hear it.

Rosie, Dawn and Emma had noticed how Lizzy was isolating herself and Rosie kindly offered to omit her lines from the script – she said the other girls could take on all the speaking parts. That way, she'd explained, Lizzy didn't need to join in the rehearsals with the Ouija board, as they were clearly upsetting for her. Lizzy would simply join them on the actual performance, knowing where she needed to be standing and how she should react to the dialogue. This took the pressure off immensely and Lizzy appreciated the time to herself whilst her friends were rehearsing.

Lizzy found that the tiredness from lack of sleep was impacting everything. During the first rehearsal that she didn't need to attend, she had decided to take a nap. Somehow sleeping in the day felt less unnerving than at night. As she settled beneath her covers though, she couldn't shake the feeling that she was being watched – again, from the window. She settled her mind by assuring herself that it was a trauma response from her scary delusion of seeing a face at the changing room window that night. As time swept her further away from that moment, she chose to believe it was a hallucination brought on by her fever. This is what she told herself as she fell into a tentative sleep afternoon. She was crudely awoken by her bedclothes slowly creeping their way down off her chest, along her legs and dropping to the floor, as though somebody at the foot of the bed was gradually revealing her sleeping body, removing the duvet cautiously so as not to wake her…she was fully aware of the sensation, but was too frightened to open her eyes. She was so scared the man would be standing there. When she finally summoned the courage to open them, there was no-one there – the room was still and a cold, blue-tinged light from the December day gave the room a calm quality. It was *possible*, Lizzy told herself, that she had just dreamt it and kicked off her own covers. She scrambled to the foot of the bed to gather her duvet upon her again and struggled her way back into sleep, but before she could get there, the covers were violently yanked off her and thrown against the far wall. Lizzy screamed, jumped up and ran from the room.

After that, she spent rehearsal times wandering in the grounds, wrapped up in coat, hat, gloves and scarf. She felt strangely drawn to the rose garden, which – in December – was nothing but twigs and thorns. She could still smell the roses though, always.

One afternoon, she passed by the potting shed and peered in. She sheltered her face by cupping her palms, casting shadow to see in – it was just a usual shed; gloomy, with shelves of the expected tools and gardening paraphernalia. But as she shrugged at the normality of it, she felt somebody breathe warm breath at her ear, through the cold, stark December air. She turned quickly thinking one of her friends had snuck up on her, but there was nobody there. She shivered and returned to the house, biting back tears. It seemed she was plagued wherever she went.

Vickie had taken annual leave for a few days for an 'early family Christmas' since her sister was visiting from Australia, but would be flying home to Brisbane before Christmas eve. It had been a happy time – never relaxing but spirited and light all the same. She returned to the school feeling concerned though – that the day before she left, she had offered her support to Lizzy regarding the upsetting paranormal episodes she seemed to be experiencing, and then totally forgot to mention that she would be away for a few days. It had bothered her whilst she'd been away and so she made it her priority to speak with Lizzy at the first opportunity as soon as she was back. She had summoned her to her study and had a mug of hot chocolate waiting for her, with the obligatory marshmallows floating on top.

"Am I in some sort of trouble?" Lizzy asked, eyes full of concern as she poked her head around Vickie's door.

"Of course not!" Vickie laughed and bundled her into the armchair, "Hot choccy!" Vickie announced as she handed Lizzy the mug.

Lizzy smiled for what felt like the first time in a while, "mmm, thank you..."

"I've been away on leave," Vickie announced apologetically, "and I'm so sorry – I should have told you I was going away, after I'd promised to be there for you...how have you been?"

Lizzy shrugged, "Okay, I suppose." In truth, she hadn't noticed Vickie's absence – she didn't feel like she noticed much nowadays about anything much.

"And the things you couldn't tell me before in case they got your friends in trouble. Has anything changed there?" Vickie prompted.

Lizzy hesitated. It occurred to her that tonight it was the evening of the Christmas play performances

– the 'big reveal night' as Rosie insisted upon calling it. Tonight, everybody would know about their secretive prop anyway. After this evening, the whole Ouija board fiasco would be a thing of the past – it couldn't hurt to tell Vickie about it now. It would certainly help Lizzy to talk about the whole thing. She took a deep breath.

"You know our play is a ghost story?" Lizzy began.

"Yes," nodded Vickie, manoeuvring herself into the seat opposite Lizzy.

"And that weird spooky stuff has been happening – specifically to me – since we started rehearsing?" Lizzy built up to it.

Vickie nodded.

"Well, I distinctly believe that the *reason* things have begun getting strange is that our *prop* may have awoken things..." Lizzy looked at her hot chocolate as she spoke.

"Ah. Mrs Stevens told me your prop was a secret – I don't suppose you can tell me what it is now?" Vickie asked, coyly.

"We found a Ouija board in the props cupboard," Lizzy said it quickly to get it out of the way.

Vickie sat forward with a start, her face blanching in alarm.

"I didn't think we should use it, but Em...I mean, some of the other girls thought it would be fun." Once Lizzy started telling the story of it, she couldn't stop, "And they wrote a whole play around it, and we promised each other we wouldn't *actually use* the board; we agreed not to play it. But a couple of the girls...well, they tried it out even though we agreed, and they didn't really know what they were doing and they didn't 'shut it down' properly or something...?"

"They didn't say '*goodbye*' on the board?" Vickie whispered.

"That's it – they didn't say *goodbye*..." Lizzy confirmed, "you sound like you know something about Ouija boards?"

"I'm Irish, sweetheart – we know a thing or two about the spirit world," Vickie forced a small smile, "but tell me this – now this is very important; the time they failed to say *goodbye*, had they been in conversation with any spirits?"

Lizzy recalled that day – the way Emma and Dawn had feigned normality and rushed off, then only later revealed that they had indeed been talking to something which had correctly called out the names Rosemary and Clara. That the whatever-it-was 'talking' to them had claimed to be killed by Clara.

Lizzy nodded, "Yes, I believe they had been talking to something."

Vickie breathed in quickly and ran her hands down her face, "Tell me they're not still using the board in the play?"

"They are – the whole play is based around the board," Lizzy explained.

"They'll have to change the play," Vickie stated.

"But the play is *tonight!* There's no way they can change it now..." Lizzy protested, getting flustered, "and Rosie – Vickie, you know Rosie is trying to prove to her parents that they should allow her to go into acting instead of studying Medicine. Tonight is her big opportunity; she's desperate to showcase what she can do to the school so that her teachers get behind her and encourage her into acting."

Vickie sighed, sinking down and shaking her head, "I need to burn the board" she muttered.

"Burn the board?" Lizzy couldn't quite believe that a fully-grown adult was taking this seriously.

Vickie nodded firmly "It's the only solution to getting rid of what is quite obviously hanging around.

Having been away for a few days, the atmosphere when I walked back into Holly House was thick with it. The smell of roses in the corridor is stronger, the singing in the post-room is louder, the – I don't know what it is – a dark, ugly *presence* is just smothering the place," Vickie paused and narrowed her eyes at Lizzy, "you feel it too."

Lizzy's eyes filled with tears, "Yes. It's horrible. I can't sleep. But the whole time I'm awake, I feel it. I can't get away from it."

"And you don't want it to follow you home for Christmas...?" Vickie lifted an eyebrow.

"God, no!" Lizzy panicked.

"Then I have to burn the board," Vickie insisted, kindly.

"Just.... *after* the show? Please don't let me have ruined this for everyone else. Please just wait until the play is done?" Lizzy pleaded with her.

Vickie took a moment, and then against her better judgement, closed her eyes and acquiesced with a reluctant nod.

"Tell me what happens in the play, so if things are going off-track, I can shut it down," Vickie instructed.

"Rosie will kill me if I tell you the spoiler..." Lizzy attempted.

"It's that or I confiscate the board now and burn it – that's what I *should* be doing..."

"Okay, okay!" Lizzy held up her palms in defence, "so the play goes that three girls find the Ouija board and decide to use it for their play, they learn how to use the board, start to play it and then there is a jump-scare moment where a matron appears behind the audience to yell '*Get to your rooms!*'" Lizzy spread her hands signalling that concluded the synopsis and Vickie nodded her head unhappily then held out her hand to take Lizzy's empty mug.

"You're cross with me," Lizzy observed.

"I'm not cross with *you*," Vickie clarified, "I'm disturbed by what had been dredged up here and I'm uncomfortable with the whole situation."

"I'm sorry..." Lizzy said, genuinely feeling it, "for my part in it, I am so sorry."

Vickie opened her arms to hug Lizzy and Lizzy happily stepped into the embrace, welcoming Vickie's support and affection.

"If anything seems odd, before the performance or during it – you let me know? I'll burn the board after the show tonight." Vickie reminded her.

"Okay," Lizzy agreed, sincerely hoping she wouldn't have any need to reach out to Vickie.

Tomorrow would be the Christmas party and packing-up day before going home to her grandmother for the Christmas break. There was even talk of her parents possibly being able to join them from abroad for Christmas this year – she really hoped so. The end of this awful episode was in sight – they just needed to get through tonight.

CHAPTER 12
1875

Clara had waited all evening until the house seemed quiet enough that she could go and knock on the potting shed door. Even though she knew that George had no idea she had doubted him, the guilt at having believed such terrible things regarding his character made her want to give herself completely to him. She tiptoed hastily down the stairs and along the corridor, holding her lantern. She could smell Rosemary's darn rose perfume and so turned to the post room just to check that she wasn't lingering anywhere – and as she faced the pigeon-holes, she noticed that all were empty apart from two of them. One was Betty's... the paper looked thin and before

Clara could question what she was doing, she lifted the note and unfolded it.

It was unmistakably George's handwriting, and it read:

B. I will not rest until I have you. You are mine.

With a sharp intake of breath, Clara's hand flew to her chest. All her fears materialised in that one note. Yet – there was another note that looked similar in another pigeon-hole; that of Ada Woods. Clara didn't care anymore; she reached for it – George's handwriting again:

Do you like wine? I have some for you for Christmas. You know where to find me.

Clara's breath caught in her throat. She couldn't believe the betrayal of this repugnant man and his repulsive tendencies were now entirely clear to her. She took a deep breath and marched to the dining room door – she was still going to knock for him, but instead of falling into his arms, she planned on slapping him across his vile, lying face.

She stormed at the dining room door; it was always stiff and noisy to open but right now it would not shift at all. She flung herself against it but it was as if there was something stopping it from moving on the other side. Clara peered down through the glass and was horrified to find that there was a mound of something – some*one* lying against it. For a split second, she hoped it was the abhorrent George Stone, dying of a heart attack. But as her eyes adjusted, she could see long hair and she recognised the frill of the edge of the apron. No... It couldn't be Rosemary! A strangled sob escaped Clara's mouth as she covered her face and ran back to her room. There, she quickly retrieved the unread letter from Betty from her top drawer and ripped into it. She sat shaking as she read how the man, she had believed to be her lover had stalked, terrorised and assaulted this young girl. And Clara – the gatekeeper to the children – had enabled him to do so. Rosemary had attempted to support Betty. She had tried to help, and Clara had punished her for it. Now Rosemary was dead – or if not dead, certainly very hurt. Clara knew she should go back down, investigate whether Rosemary might still be alive and in need of medical treatment. But Clara Brown was a coward. Clara Brown buried herself under her bedclothes and left the body of Rosemary Faulkner out in the below-freezing temperatures to be discovered in the morning, stiff and covered in frost.

CHAPTER 13
PRESENT DAY

The excitement backstage was contagious. Even Lizzy felt the surge of happy energy – various girls peeked around the red velvet curtains, looking out at the other children in the audience who were there to watch. With the recreation hall lights dimmed and only the stage lit, students hurried about making final preparations, animated with heightened anticipation.

The first play revolved around a toy soldier that was the selected prop – it was essentially a condensed version of the Nutcracker which, whilst festive, Rosie turned her nose up at, labelling it plagiarism. The audience though were enraptured and the enthusiasm in the room was electric.

Rosie, Lizzy, Emma and Dawn were up next.

There was such a buzz and thrill about the event. Rosie in particular was giddy with nervous excitement, "I just can't wait for the jump-scare!" she whispered to the others, and they all giggled in shared anticipation – even Lizzy, who was so relieved that, after this, normal life might resume. In the half-light behind the stage curtain, they set the table, and Dawn grabbed the Ouija board, ready to begin.

"The big reveal! People will *finally* know what our secret prop is!" Emma squealed. The girls all giggled in a huddle, then Rosie hugged each of them and announced "Showtime!"

IN THE OPENING SCENE, the tension in the darkness was tangible. As the girls ventured out of the hole under the stage, with torches under their faces, their audience was so silent nobody dare even sniff. Then the moment that Rosie's character shone the torch onto the Ouija board announcing, "*I found THIS!*" the audience gasped at the realisation of what it was and then there were uncomfortable giggles and excited whispers from the crowd.

Rosie allowed them to settle before continuing with the dialogue, in which the characters squabbled over whether or not they should use the Ouija board as a prop for their play. Lizzy – who was not as engaged in her acting as the likes of Rosie – found herself wondering how Mrs Stevens was feeling about the Ouija board reveal and whether they might be in trouble later that evening.

The curtain rose on the scene of the Ouija board game. Lizzy's heart fluttered as she took her seat, in character, on stage at the Ouija board, about to place her fingers on the glass. This felt incredibly uncomfortable but at least this time her friends would have to stick to the script.

The audience were rigid in their silence; every spectator nervous and primed to be shocked. Rosie owned the stage – loving each moment that the audience hung on to her every word. She spoke her character's lines clearly and slowly *"If anybody is there...let us know. Would any spirits like to connect with us?"*

The glass began to move. The script required them to spell out 'H.E.L.L.O.'

But the glass moved towards the 'B.'

"No," Lizzy couldn't help herself saying. Rosie flicked her a warning look, which reprimanded her for going off-script in the actual performance, but

Dawn looked panicked too, realising that this was none of them messing about.

Rosie made the impulsive decision to read the dialogue as it was scripted, since the audience probably couldn't see what letters the glass was going to anyway.

"H.E.L..." Rosie began, but it was futile – the glass was now whizzing around the board with aggressive force and Lizzy watched as it continued "B.E.T.T.Y.B.E.T.T.Y.B.E.T"

Rosie was overwhelmed by the velocity of the glass and couldn't go on with her script. She floundered and as she stopped speaking, the table the board was on began to tremble, as if somebody was literally standing there, shaking it with both hands. Lizzy shrieked and she was aware of nervous laughter from the children in the audience, who clearly believed this was part of the narrative.

Rosie and Dawn were still trying to get the glass under control, when it suddenly lifted and smashed onto the stage. All three girls onstage stood and gasped, backing off from the glass. Some of the audience clapped and reacted in gasps at how realistic the production was.

Then the table began to lift off the floor and slammed back down. Then up and again, slamming back down. Lizzy couldn't believe her eyes as she watched it levitate. The crowd seemed to collectively take a breath and applause broke out at what they assumed to be an incredible special effect. The table continued to lift then until it was at head-height. Lizzy remembered that Vickie had told her she should reach out to her if things went off-script. She expected that by now, Vickie had probably realised this was *not* part of the play, but she yelled out regardless, "Vickie! Help!"

At that moment, the table flipped and was thrown, by some invisible force, off the stage towards the audience. The girls on stage screamed at the realisation the situation was now totally out of control and people could actually get hurt. The table luckily landed in the centre of the aisle between the seats and as a result, the perplexed audience still didn't fathom that the cast were no longer in control of the play. Some screamed with shock, a few of the younger ones could be heard crying but the majority laughed in delighted surprise at this exciting turn of events.

Then – the moment that Emma should appear at the back of the hall and bellow, acting as the matron, there was a loud booming voice from the back of the hall, but it was not Emma's voice. This was a man's voice; deep, angry, other-worldly in its rich clarity. Every person in the hall heard it at a volume as if the man had been shouting directly in their ear. It was painful to hear and as every single person in the hall turned their immediate attention to the back of the hall, they saw an extremely tall man with a shock of dark hair, leathery skin and black eyes. He was pointing at the stage and shouting "YOU ARE MINE!!"

Then – he faded in to thin air in front of their eyes and behind him stood the shaken, pale Emma, looking tiny in comparison to this giant of an apparition.

It was at this point that the children in the audience began to audibly cry and panic. Teachers fussed about to try and stop what was happening.

"Stop!" bellowed Mrs Stevens, running down the aisle towards the stage, dodging the broken thrown table, "Stop the play!"

"We've stopped..." Rosie whimpered. Lizzy fell to her knees, shaking all over. She knew the man's pointing hand had been directly at her.

The staff ushered all the children from the audience quickly out of the recreation hall and into the main entranceway and Mrs Stevens ushered the girls quickly off the stage into the dining room, where she followed and yelled "What the HELL did you think you were doing!?"

All the girls were ashen-faced, and Rosie tried to justify, "That wasn't the play we planned Mrs Stevens...it went...we didn't..."

"A Ouija Board!?" Mrs Stevens screeched, "You KNEW I wouldn't have allowed it! That's why you kept it a secret! I *trusted* you! You have wreaked havoc on the place. Frightened everybody half-to-death, nearly harmed the children in the audience and trashed school property! I have a good mind to expel you all right here on the spot!"

Dawn attempted to placate her next, "We didn't mean for any of that to happen, Mrs Stevens...the board took over – there's a spirit..."

"Don't you dare try to place the blame elsewhere!" Mrs Stevens began even though she was clearly shaken from the experience and aware that this could not be exclusively the girls' own doing, but then Emma interrupted,

"Where's Lizzy?"

They all stopped and looked about the room in concern, then Emma ran back to the stage of the recreation room, where she found Lizzy lying on the stage, sobbing uncontrollably.

"Help!" Emma cried out and Vickie came running.

"Oh, God help us!" Vickie lifted Lizzy to carry her from the stage, "Mrs Stevens, we need the school nurse!" Vickie called out. Vickie sat her in the armchair in her office and the school nurse arrived. Taking Lizzy's hand, which was ice cold, she asked Vickie to fetch a warm blanket, a cup of sweet tea and a hot water bottle. Mrs Stevens was already on the phone to Lizzy's Grandmother.

After the commotion had died down and Lizzy was in the arms of her grandmother,

Vickie snuck out and taking a drinking glass from the servery hatch in the dining room she sloped back to the stage. She cautiously placed the glass on the board and placed it at *Goodbye*, speaking it out loud as she did so, then she folded the board and took it outside to burn in the steel bin behind the potting shed.

CHAPTER 14
1875

Clara generally enjoyed her own company. It was rare in a school-full of children to have even a moment of silence – let alone three weeks. Her sister-in-law, Alice, had invited her to spend Christmas day with the Brown family, but the rest of the time, Clara was here, at the empty school, in her quiet apartment, with little to occupy her mind.

Christmas day had been fine – but she had felt very much an outsider, a guest. When Clara's husband Damien had been alive, they would be invited together to spend Christmas eve with his sister's family; to experience the children opening their presents Christmas morning and sometimes even to stay over on Christmas night if they all became too merry to reasonably make the journey home. In those times, it had been relaxed and – although she hadn't properly appreciated it at the time – she had been embraced as a family member. Now she was invited for 10am – after the children had enjoyed their present opening and the Browns booked a coach to bring her back to Holly House at 6pm, directly after the early dinner. She had felt a little put-out that they didn't offer to make up a room for her in their huge extensive house, but concluded, with sadness, that she was now regarded as a visitor and not as one who belonged. She moped about in this self-pity for a few days but knew that it was exacerbated by the huge revelations she had been hit with in her personal life.

Upon realising that George Stone had been messaging young girls and inviting them to drink alcohol with him, along with the stark reality that Betty's accusations were likely based in truth, she had also heard Julie and a pantry-girl discussing taking a torn dress to Susannah Stone, the seamstress in the village. Clara had interrupted to ask who it was that they spoke of, and they confirmed they were talking about George Stone's wife.

"But she died?" Clara asked, blinking her eyes double-quick-time.

The two women looked at each other and shook their heads.

"No, Mrs Stevens," Julie informed her, "she is very well and a wonderful seamstress, though she hasn't been taking as much work on since she had the baby…"

Clara didn't grace this revelation with a response – she wasn't sure she could retain composure in front of her junior colleagues, so she just walked away and processed this additional heartbreak in the privacy of her apartment, feigning a headache for the remainder of the day.

Now, here she was alone in this large boarding house, devastated over her loss of George – the man she thought her future would revolve around, the anger at his many betrayals festering inside of her, the realisation that she now belonged nowhere, with no-one and then… the sickening issue she tried not to think about. The death of Rosemary Faulkner.

The whole school had fallen into grief upon the news that Rosemary had fallen from a window – the upper echelons who were privy to the information that she had been dismissed from her position and that it was likely suicide, agreed to keep this part quiet, out of respect for the dead and additionally so as to not assume any blame upon the school for the way the situation had been dealt with.

Nobody but Clara knew the truth – that she had framed Rosemary, who was only trying to make positive change and protect the students from a predator. Clara knew the guilt was brimming just below the surface but if she didn't look at it, she wouldn't have to think about it and she could just move on with her life with nobody knowing what really happened.

The one thing Clara *did* need to decide upon was how to disseminate the information she now knew about George. The death of Rosemary and the end of term had come thick and fast upon each other, and with medical and police matters to be dealt with and children to be packed up and shipped out, there was no moment available for her to consider how to approach reporting George Stone. She had told herself that she would deal with it in the new year – but that was now fast approaching, and she still didn't know what to do.

George had kept a wide berth in the aftermath of Rosemary's demise and Clara had wondered if he might pay her a visit over the Christmas break – and whether she would be brave enough to confront him whilst there was nobody else here to support her should he turn nasty. But he hadn't appeared. He must be with his wife and baby in the village, she thought bitterly. His absence spelled the end of their romance even if it had not been officially stated. The more she thought about it, she considered it would be safer perhaps to go straight to Alice and report George, instead of confronting him herself. That way she could hide behind the authorities and would never have to deal with him face-to-face.

But what if George countered her accusation by revealing their relationship? This would compromise her position, her status and her lovely apartment – she couldn't have it. Did he have any evidence of their union? She had never written him any notes, but she didn't trust that he wouldn't have taken some underwear or a possession of some sort. Clara decided to visit his potting shed to remove any suggestion of her dalliance with George Stone. Clara reached the dining room – she had purposely avoided this door since the night she found Rosemary's body heaped against it and she couldn't bear to take that direction even now, so she diverted through the pantry and the laundry room and out the back entrance, where the matrons would always hang the washing on the line. Why could she still smell Rosemary's blasted rose scent? The roses certainly weren't blooming in the depths of December. She shook her head to rid herself of it and marched across the lawn to the potting shed.

George didn't lock the shed door, so she let herself in with ease and started picking her way through his things. She could smell him strongly in here – the earthiness of him, and his sweat, which she had once found strangely intoxicating, now made her want to wretch. There was also a smell of stale alcohol and Clara noticed, on his small table, there was a wine glass with the remnants of red wine in the bottom. But George didn't drink wine – he only drank ale and gin. Beside the glass was an exercise book – with a shaking hand, Clara reached out to open it and saw on the opening page the name 'Ada Woods' written in ink. Ada Woods had been in this potting shed drinking with George Stone! Clara felt an anger rise inside her, like a volcano about to erupt. She had no way to express her absolute fury at this disgusting man who had a wife and baby girl, as well as a lover and yet still pursued young girls. If he had been there in front of her at the very moment, she would have willingly grabbed the pitchfork that leaned against the shed wall and stabbed him with it. But he wasn't there, he hadn't come back to visit her as he had promised, knowing she was alone over Christmas and New Year. Well, she knew what she must do, he wasn't going to get away with it.

CHAPTER 15
PRESENT DAY

Lizzy sat herself up in bed and plumped the soft cushions behind her. Her Grandma Eliza had kindly left the curtains open as she napped, so that when she woke, she could see her favourite view across the fields. It was more picturesque in the summer, when the rapeseed fields were in bloom, but now in winter, she could see a horse cantering in one of the paddocks across the way. It made her smile, and she felt safe for the first time in weeks. Grandma Eliza pushed open her bedroom door with a tray and cooed, "Ooh, you're awake! Lovely to see you looking a bit healthier!" On the tray was a glass of orange juice and a croissant with strawberry jam. Lizzy suddenly felt famished and started tucking in.

They hadn't yet spoken about anything that had happened at the school. The doctor had left Eliza instructions to just let Lizzy rest – her body and her mind. But it seemed, as her grandma took the seat next to the bed and sighed, that now was the time to talk.

"So, what do you want to tell me?" Grandma Eliza patted Lizzy's arm affectionately.

"Anything I tell you will make you think I'm mad," Lizzy declared sullenly.

"Why don't you try me out?" Eliza encouraged.

Lizzy swallowed down a delicious mouthful of buttery croissant and took a deep breath.

"We had to devise a play for the Christmas productions. The idea is that you choose a prop and use that as inspiration for your play's theme. Emma chose a Ouija board."

Grandma Eliza blinked slowly, with a sad smile - she had obviously already been told this detail.

"Emma and Dawn tried the board out, even though we'd all agreed we wouldn't use it, that we would only pretend to play it as we acted. A spirit contacted them, apparently. Started saying things about 'Betty' and 'Rosemary' and how 'Clara' killed Rosemary. All sorts of weird stuff but basically, they didn't sign off the board the way you're supposed to, and Rosie says that if you don't do that, the spirits stay around."

Lizzy paused to sip her orange juice and see how her grandma was reacting to what she was saying. Grandma Eliza was poker-faced, just listening, so Lizzy continued.

"It seems like whatever this spirit thing was, fixated on me. Whenever we tried to rehearse the play with the board it would start asking about a 'Betty'. Notes started appearing in my pigeon-hole..." At this, Grandma Eliza drew in a sharp breath, then nodded apologetically for Lizzy to continue.

"I kept feeling like I was being watched and feeling cold shivers, shadows passing by the windows...then one night, my duvet was ripped off me while I slept – that happened again just the other day while I napped. I saw a man's face at the window of the second-floor changing room, looking in at me. The spirit on the board knew about something I'd done when nobody else was around to witness it...that was so weird. I kept smelling roses and hearing humming and singing in the postal corridor. And then the night of the play, something completely took over control of the board and smashed the glass we were using on the stage, lifted the table into the air and threw it into the audience. Then he appeared – the man I'd seen in the window, and he yelled and *everyone there* saw him and heard him..." Lizzy took a breath and a bite of her croissant, then laid back against her pillow, relieved she'd said it all.

Her Grandma looked quite pale. Not shocked; Lizzy was sure Mrs Stevens or Vickie would have told her some of the things she had revealed. But Grandma Eliza was processing all this and then she placed her hand on Lizzy's arm.

"What is your name?" Grandma Eliza asked softly.

Lizzy frowned at this strange question but knew her Grandma Eliza well enough to trust she would be leading somewhere relevant, so she played along. "Lizzy."

Grandma Eliza nodded. "Why are you called Lizzy?"

"After you," Lizzy nodded assertively, "we're both Elizabeth."

"Exactly, and we are both named after your great-grandmother," Grandma Eliza explained "my mother."

"Was she was called Lizzy too?" Lizzy asked innocently.

"She was also Elizabeth, but people called her Betty, another shortened version of the name," Grandma Eliza declared and then watched as her granddaughter connected the dots in her mind.

"Betty was the name the spirit kept trying to contact!" she almost whispered as the penny seemed to drop.

"Then he *was* after me! He kept saying my name!" Lizzy found it all the more frightening that the whole time the spirit had been saying *her* name and she hadn't even known.

"Not quite" Grandma Eliza continued,

"My mother – your great grandmother, Betty – she was also a pupil at Meadowbank School for Girls, did you know?"

Lizzy narrowed her eyes, sensing pieces coming together and unsure she would like what she would hear.

"Class of 1875 – a long time ago...she looked exactly like you. Long red hair, pale complexion, piercing blue eyes..." Grandma Eliza smoothed her hand over Lizzy's flushed cheek as she described her. "You have seen her in the photo downstairs on the piano, the old black and white one with me as a baby, do you remember it?"

"Yes of course, you are in that huge pram," said Lizzy,

"that's right, well my mum, Betty, she had some trouble at the school," Grandma Eliza dropped her eyeline. "The gardener there, a bad man, he developed an unhealthy obsession with her. He would – leave her notes in her postal pigeon-hole..." Grandma Eliza paused for Lizzy to compute.

Lizzy's hand went quickly to cover her mouth, and her eyes were wide with shock.

"He'd invite her to drink wine with him in his potting shed; the same one that still stands there today..." Lizzy let out an involuntary gasp as this all sounded so familiar.

"My mother told me all this when I was a teenager – she wanted me to be aware of predatory men. She learnt quite a few lessons that year about bullies and bad adults. She talked me through everything that happened to her so that she could pass on her wisdom. She told me this bad man – he was even spotted by the girls at the changing room window, peering through looking at them as they dressed..." Eliza had known this would shake Lizzy the most and was ready with another hug as tears started to flood down Lizzy's cheeks.

"I thought I was going mad!" Lizzy blurted through the tears, "But all the time, it was *really happening!* I don't know what's worse..."

Eliza smoothed Lizzy's hair, "Your matron, Vickie, she burnt the Ouija board, and Holly House has been blessed by the vicar too. He won't be bothering you anymore."

"But who were the other names he mentioned? Clara – he said Clara killed him? And Rosemary?"

Grandma Eliza nodded and composed herself for the next part of the story.

"Rosemary was a lovely matron in Holly House– she was the wonderful lady who supported your Great Grandma Betty through the situation with the awful gardener. She was known for making beautiful rose perfume and for always singing and humming down the corridor -" Lizzy's mouth fell open in shock.

"Yes, I know," Grandma Eliza acknowledged. "Rosemary had a plan to report George Stone, the Gardener, for harassing young students. But she died before she had the chance."

"No!" Lizzy exclaimed.

"It was rumoured that the gardener was also

having a love affair with the housemistress, named Clara..."

"Clara!" Lizzy recognised the name and Eliza nodded, "the spirit said Clara killed Rosemary?"

"That was what was suspected," Grandma Eliza confirmed, "Rosemary's death was officially classed as a suicide, but the events that led towards her fall from the top floor may have been carefully orchestrated by Clara, as she didn't want Rosemary to report George Stone, her lover."

"But the spirit – I assume that was this George Stone – he also said that Clara killed *him?*"

"That's interesting. Grandma Betty said his death was inconclusive, but that once it was discovered what he had been doing and his inappropriate interest in the girls, nobody had much interest in finding out how he had died. I think everybody was just rather relieved he wasn't around anymore. But as the spirit of George Stone has quite undeniably made his presence known from beyond the grave and says that is what happened, I'm rather inclined to believe it..."

CHAPTER 16
1876

Clara had watched from the window as they removed George Stones' body from the potting shed. They thought he may have accidentally ingested some weedkiller – nobody could fathom how he had managed to get it into ale, but once they found the distasteful pile of materials stacked on his desk, nobody bothered looking into it much further. There was a pile of notes written by him that were full of messages inciting the reader to visit him; to drink with him...they were sat next to an exercise book belonging to Ada Woods from Year 9. And in the bin, was a balled-up letter, written by Betty Grainger from year 10, reporting George Stone for a variety of disgusting predatory behaviours. It was addressed to Mrs Brown, the headmistress, but had somehow turned up in George Stone's bin instead. After these findings, the police considered he had killed himself, unable to accept what a vile human being he was, and the case was closed.

Clara could smell roses whenever she walked down the corridor and often heard singing and humming as she sorted the post. She saw the back of Rosemary's dress disappear around the door of the dining room late one night and she vowed never to go downstairs at night again. She retreated to her rooms in the afternoons and became distant with her staff and the girls. Her sister-in-law, Alice, called Clara to her office to discuss her lack of motivation and apparent loss of interest in her work. Clara couldn't summon the energy to deny her apathy and listlessness. She told Alice she was being haunted by the spirit of Rosemary Faulkner, to which Alice told her she needed to see the doctor for her hallucinations.

Late January, as Clara closed her curtains one night, she saw George Stone standing on the lawn looking up at her with a deadly sneer across his white face and evil in his black eyes. She fell backwards in horror the first time. It happened most nights from then, but each time she saw him he was closer and closer to the dining room door.

In February, as she hurried the girls to dress in the changing rooms after their sports lessons in time for assembly, Clara screamed and fainted when she saw George Stone's face at the window peering in at her.

In March, it snowed, and Clara discovered large, heavy-set men's boot-prints leading towards the dining room doors through the snow from the potting shed. Nobody had yet taken over the Gardener's role and the only man employed at Holly House was the warden, who was strongly superstitious and refused to step foot anywhere near the potting shed.

In April, Clara felt her bed covers being pulled from her bed and woke with a start to find George Stone towering above her, his hands wrapped tightly around her neck. Her screams woke the whole house and the doctor was called.

In May, Alice Brown and her husband arrived at Clara's apartment to help her pack her things. She sat on the edge of her bed, wearing her nightclothes rocking gently back and forth, humming to herself as they packed up bags around her. Julie watched as the doctor helped Clara into the carriage and instructed the driver to take them to the asylum.

Newspaper advertisements publicised vacancies for a Housemistress, Matron and Gardener for Holly House at Meadowbank School. Mrs Brown never mentioned her sister-in-law again.

THE END.

ALSO BY CHARLOTTE WEBB

The Lighthouse - A Ghost Story

The lighthouse cottage stands on a windswept cliff, surrounded by breathtaking views of sea and sky—a place where time seems to stand still. Its beauty feels almost otherworldly, a tranquil haven far removed from the chaos of modern life. But beneath its serene surface lies something far darker, an unseen force rooted in the cottage's tragic past.

For Emily, the new resident, the ghosts of the past are not just echoes or fleeting memories. They begin as whispers on the wind, cold spots in the cozy cottage, and flickering lights in the dead of night. At first, the disturbances seem harmless, even explainable. But as the weeks pass, they become more invasive, slipping into her dreams and, eventually, her waking life. When the hauntings turn physical, Emily realises the spirits are not just restless—they're angry.

Sometimes, the ghosts of the past refuse to let go.

Read now - The Lighthouse

ABOUT THE AUTHOR

You are warmly invited to download Charlotte's first, free little book, and to connect with her on Facebook.

Here you can keep up to date with new releases and join in to chat about everything spooky and paranormal.

Ravencross Road (Download for free)

Facebook Page (Please like and follow)

Facebook Group - Charlotte's Haunted House

Charlotte Webb is a gifted author with a passion for all things paranormal. Her love for ghosts and the supernatural led her to run a business in the UK, taking curious thrill-seekers to haunted locations steeped in mystery. With firsthand experiences in some of the country's most eerie sites, Charlotte brings a vivid authenticity to her writing, drawing readers into chilling tales that feel all too real. Her books weave fact and fiction seamlessly, blending her encounters with an imagination that knows no bounds, offering readers a window into the worlds where shadows move, secrets linger, and the past never truly fades away.

Charlotte now resides in an old cottage in a small Northamptonshire village which is steeped in history and holds many ghost stories of its own. She shares her home with her husband, five rescue dogs, four parrots, and a lively flock of chickens and ducks. One of her books is set in this very home, and tells the story of a true ghostly character that has been seen many times in the countryside around her cottage.

Can you tell which is fact or fiction?

Printed in Great Britain
by Amazon